351 Practical Ways to Save Money Now!

The Little Book of
Big
Savings

- Put money in your pocket with 15-minute tips!
- Reclaim lost dollars in 12 spending categories!
- Save $1200 each month from household bills!

ELLIE KAY

author of *Living Rich for Less*,
America's Family Financial Expert®

D0651002

THE LITTLE BOOK OF BIG SAVINGS
PUBLISHED BY WATERBROOK PRESS
12265 Oracle Boulevard, Suite 200
Colorado Springs, Colorado 80921

Details in some anecdotes and stories have been changed to protect the
identities of the persons involved.

ISBN 978-0-307-45861-2
ISBN 978-0-307-45880-3 (electronic)

Published in the United States by WaterBrook Multnomah, an imprint of the
Crown Publishing Group, a division of Random House Inc., New York.

WATERBROOK and its deer colophon are registered trademarks of Random
House Inc.

Library of Congress Cataloging-in-Publication Data
Kay, Ellie.
    The little book of big savings : 351 practical ways to save money now! /
Ellie Kay.—1st ed.
        p. cm.
Includes bibliographical references.
    ISBN 978-0-307-45861-2—ISBN 978-0-307-45880-3 (electronic)
1. Finance, Personal. 2. Budgets, Personal. 3. Consumer education. 4. Saving
and investment. I. Title.
    HG179.K37887 2009
    332.024—dc22

                                            2009023107

Printed in the United States of America
2009—First Edition

10 9 8 7 6 5 4 3 2 1

SPECIAL SALES
Most WaterBrook Multnomah books are available at special quantity discounts
when purchased in bulk by corporations, organizations, and special-interest
groups. Custom imprinting or excerpting can also be done to fit special needs.
For information, please e-mail SpecialMarkets@WaterBrookMultnomah.com
or call 1-800-603-7051.

~

To the Three Graces

Audrey Dick, a prophet in the making
Brenda Taylor, a forever friend
Madeline Brazell, Amigita Mia

Contents

1

Surprise! You Have More Money Than You Thought You Had!

Some of my most exciting moments are when I find unexpected "surprise" money. You know the kind. While cleaning out the pockets before you throw your jeans in the washing machine, you pull out a five dollar bill you forgot you had. Or when you're walking down the street and you discover a dollar bill just lying there.

It's the best feeling, isn't it?

Well, what if I were to tell you that you have surprise money all around you. In every room of your house or apartment. Money just sitting there, waiting for you to notice it. Yes, you read that right!

You just have to know where and how to look.

Extra cash. Even if you've lost your job. Even if you are so far in debt that you see everything in red. Even if your family is eating you out of house and home.

How do I know you can find money right under your nose? Because when my husband, Bob, and I were first married, we were $40,000 in consumer debt—and yet everywhere I looked, I realized that I could find money. I felt so empowered! And within two and a half years, living on just my husband's military salary, we used all that surprise money to pay off our debts.

Fifteen years and seven children later, we were able to pay cash for our cars (we even gave away three cars!), buy and nicely furnish two five-bedroom houses (moving from one to the other), take wonderful vacations, dress our family in style, build a nest egg for retirement, become debt free, and send three children (so far) to college without college loans. And the best part? My family and I have been able to share our money (more than $100,000) with people and causes that desperately need help. If a military husband, a stay-at-home mom, and seven kids can do it, believe me, so can you!

I'm passionate about saving money, and I'm really good at it (if I do say so!). I can find the smartest and least expensive way to do or have just about anything. And I'm excited about being able to share all my tips with you so that you can save money too.

Yeah, right, I can hear you thinking. *I get it. My surprise money is me reusing aluminum foil over and over.* Um, no.

One time I had a woman approach me, shaking her head. She said, "Ellie, are you going to tell me I have to wash out and reuse plastic baggies?"

I'll tell you what I told her. "No! No! No! Unless…you really want to."

Hello? You don't have to live like an obsessive Scrooge in order to save money! Why do we put all these downers on saving money?

Sometimes pinching pennies can get old.

Real old.

Way old.

Big-time old.

Stinkin' old.

Big, fat, double-dog-ugly old.

Which brings me to an important point: too many people think that to save money, you have to live like a monk, taking a vow of poverty, or you have to do extreme, crazy things. Seriously. I have better ways to spend my time! And I assume you do too.

Let me put your mind at ease.

Here is a list of things I am *not* going to suggest you do in order to save money:

- Ask your grandmother to start saving foil in little balls for you.
- To save water, keep your fish in the toilet bowl and train it to cling to the sides at the first sound of rushing water.
- When at a pizza shop, and the couple next to you leaves half a pizza untouched and un-eaten, ask the waitress for a carry-out box.
- When you are driving down the road, pull over your Mercedes wannabe to pick up a piece of fruit you see lying by the side of the road.
- Search the Internet for creative ways to use those bits of soap that are too little to use but too big to throw away.
- Recycle the cotton balls that you take from the top of your vitamin bottles.
- When your friend asks you to meet her for lunch, try to talk her into a restaurant she doesn't like because it offers "buy one, get one free" and you can get the free lunch.

- Wear the same clothes three days in a row in order to "get your money's worth" out of the wash.
- Wash and reuse plastic Ziploc bags.

I'm proud of the ways my family and I—and you can!—save money. In fact, in my book *Living Rich for Less* (the companion to this book), I tell you not only how to save more than $30,000 a year by using my Cha-Ching Factor™ tips, I give you great, practical, and easy-to-implement financial principles to live a rich lifestyle. Now, does that sound like living a life filled with trained fish and aluminum foil balls?

WHAT YOU MAKE AND WHAT YOU (DON'T) SAVE

Did you know that the average American family makes $48,000 per year, and an amazing 85 percent of the population makes $100,000 or less?

Most of the average folks are living paycheck to paycheck. And in many families, ATM withdrawals account for as much as 20 percent of the month's spending, but they cannot account for a majority of those dollars! They save -0.5 percent. That means most Americans are spending more than they are making.

If you're like the average person, you don't pay attention to how much you're spending.

Your spending plan is actually, well, not a plan at all.

Take a look at the typical family, whom I'll call the Bensons. They are married with children—two, to be exact.

- They live in a modest three-bedroom, two-bath home with a yard and a lazy dog.
- They don't have a household budget.
- They have an annual income of $48,000.
- They owe about $8,500 in credit card debt.
- They have two car payments.
- They have a thirty-year mortgage.
- Their savings account has less than $500 in it.
- They have no long-term retirement account.
- They love their kids and want them to go to college.
- They are wondering, *Where did all the dough go?*

But the really amazing thing about the Bensons is where they *think* they will be one day. The Bensons believe that one day they are going to earn more money through raises or a better job. They hope they will receive an inheritance or a financial windfall. They figure that someday they will no longer have student loan payments and that childcare costs will go away when the kids are in school—thus cutting down on their monthly expenses. Then they'll finally have some breathing room. They also believe that

- One day they'll have their credit cards paid off.
- One day they'll have a nice savings account.
- One day they'll get a couple of IRAs.
- One day they will be able to send their kids to college and still have a retirement fund for their golden years.

But they have no plan! They think it will "just work out." One day, that is. One fine day.

Hello?

The hard fact about the Bensons is that if they continue the way they are now, with no real plan, they will

- Pay five times as much on their house as it is worth (possibly more with the drop in real estate prices and the economy).
- Increase their credit card debt.
- Never get out of consumer debt.
- Get a second mortgage on their home to pay for their kids' college expenses.
- Never acquire enough savings to retire comfortably.
- Always have car payments.
- Never realize their financial goals.

So much for living the American dream, right?

You may identify with the Bensons—a little too much! Or maybe you don't quite fit their profile—maybe you're not married, or married without children, or don't own a house—but you still feel their pain a little too closely.

Now may be a good time to take a good, hard, honest look at your spending habits. Ask yourself these questions—and be honest!

- Do my family and I currently live by a clear-cut, focused spending plan?
- Do I consistently stick to that plan?
- Do I buy something only because I *really* need it (not just because I want it)?
- Do I give a portion of my income to my church or a charitable cause?
- Do I have a total consumer debt load of less than 10 percent of my annual income? (For example, if you earn $50,000 per year, you have a non-mortgage debt load of $5,000 or less.)

- Do I save at least 10 percent of my income?
- Do I have a savings account with at least two months' worth of income in it?
- Do I own a retirement account or mutual fund of any kind?
- Do I buy something because a TV commercial convinces me to buy it?

As you answer those questions, you may feel, well, ill. It can be a rude awakening when someone (me!) reminds you of your situation and where you should be. That's okay.

The good news is that whatever your marital, housing, or debt situation, you can do something positive. You can change your financial future.

The key is to really pay attention to how you spend your money each month. Every month you spend your hard-earned cash on the following things: mortgage/rent and utilities, transportation, food (including dining out), clothing/dry cleaning/other shopping, recreation/entertainment, vacation, gifts, medical/dental/insurance, big-ticket items (furniture/appliances), education, pets, credit cards, savings (hopefully!), charitable giving, and other incidentals I didn't include in this list.

And every month, if you're like the Bensons, you make the payments without much thought or planning.

By picking up this book (along with my other book, *Living Rich for Less*), you've taken the first real steps to changing your future, to taking back control of where *your* money goes every month. You're going to be amazed by how much surprise money you're about to find.

In *Living Rich for Less* I go into detail about what I call a life-changing financial principle, the 10/10/80 Rule™. With this principle you give away 10 percent of your income, save 10 percent, and spend the remaining 80 percent wisely. I know people are skeptical when I tell them they need to give and save first, but when you spend the 80 percent wisely, you will more than make up for it. Trust me, I've been there, done that. I know it's possible—and I can show you how to find enough money to live rich and share your wealth.

In this book I'm going to show you exactly how to save money and spend that 80 percent wisely, so that every month you don't dread those checkbook-balancing-bill-paying moments. Can you imagine? Being thrilled and excited to balance your checkbook and see how much extra money is there?

In each of the following chapters I offer a big tip that will take about twelve minutes a week, but those minutes can pay big dividends of $1,200 a month—or more! Then I provide other great, practical tips (more than two hundred total!) that you can put into practice right away to start watching your savings grow. You'll be amazed by how much extra money you can have at the end of each month.

Ready to figure out your spending plan and put it into action? Then turn the page and let's go!

2

Save Big on Housing and Utilities

12-Minute Tip #1: When closing on a house, pay attention to lenders who tack on extra charges for services such as title search and document preparation. These can add hundreds of dollars to your closing costs and should be included in the price of title insurance, which, depending on where you live, can be as high as $6,000. Take twelve minutes to interview your lender about the specifics related to these closing costs *before* you decide to use their services. (See page 21 under "Did You Know?" for more details on how to talk with a prospective mortgage broker.) Save $1,200 or more.

Our family lived in military housing the first dozen years Bob and I were married, moving eleven times in thirteen years. By the time we were in one place long enough to buy a home, our main criteria was to make sure that the home didn't own us. This meant we needed to look hard at our credit-to-income ratio, what utilities would cost us, and then factor in general upkeep. The result was a gorgeous home that we really loved and could actually afford!

The rule of thumb is that 30 percent of your monthly payments should go toward housing and utilities, but just look at the insane numbers of foreclosures around the country and you'll see that many people are actually spending way more than 30 percent.

According to a recent study conducted by the National Association of Realtors, the average American family spends more than $1,132 a month on a mortgage, including principal and interest. That's up quite a bit from 2003 when the average monthly payment was $840.[1]

Rent isn't much better. Take a look at these major metropolitan areas and their median rents from the first quarter of 2008[2]:

Atlanta: $986
Austin: $907
Boston: $1,645
Chicago: $1,355
Las Vegas: $1,056
Los Angeles: $1,699
Miami: $1,368
New York: $1,751
Phoenix: $939
San Francisco: $1,810
Seattle: $1,211
Washington DC: $1,687

Utilities aren't much cheaper. The Consumer Expenditure Survey indicates that energy costs have risen 16.6 percent, causing the average American family to pay more than $3,600 per year in utilities.

Not surprisingly, it's taking a toll on people's finances, future security, and even family relationships. Experts are now saying that the mortgage crisis is causing an alarming number of couples to get divorced. "Faced with pressure, these couples are blaming one another!" says Scott Daniels, an Ocala, Florida, real estate agent. "Rather than attempt to work together to resolve the problem, they find it easier to separate."[3]

It's time to save your finances, future, and family relationships!

In my book *Living Rich for Less* I discuss in more depth housing and utilities issues, such as whether or not to buy, sell, downsize, or upgrade, and even include a homeowner's checklist. That companion book can help you with those details. In this chapter, though, we're going to focus on how you can save the most money by staying where you are.

❧

OVERALL MAINTENANCE

▦ Buy and use a CFL (compact fluorescent lamp) for every light bulb in your house (nine bulbs on average); save $531 over the life of the bulb.

Installing CFL bulbs is one of the easiest ways you can make an impact on your energy bills. Not only will you save money and energy, but you can pat yourself on the back that you've gone green by contributing to a cleaner environment by reducing fossil fuel usage. Modern CFL bulbs offer these benefits:

- You'll use 75 percent less energy, which saves you money (see www.energystar.gov/index .cfm?fuseaction=cal.showPledge).

- You'll save more than $30 in energy costs over the life of the bulb.
- CFL bulbs last up to ten times longer than regular light bulbs.
- CFL bulbs are available in different sizes and shapes to fit almost any fixture.

▦ Purchase products that carry the Energy Star rating on everything from hair dryers to small appliances and especially on large appliances such as refrigerators. Save up to 25 percent in energy costs.

▦ Check your windows and doors for air leaks. Use the appropriate tape to seal leaks.

▦ Have a pest-control professional inspect your home on a regular basis. If you don't, you gamble on the chance that you'll have to pay a greater expense later to debug your home, along with the potential expense of repairing structural damage.

HEATING AND COOLING

▦ Clean heating and cooling system filters regularly, and maintain heating and air conditioning units.

▦ Keep thermostats set at moderate comfort—68 to 70 degrees in winter and 74 to 78 degrees in summer. Save as much as 40 to 50 percent in hot climates and 12 percent in cooler climates.

▦ Lower the heating and cooling systems when your home is vacant for more than eight hours.

▦ Use a clock-operated thermostat so that it automatically adjusts when you aren't home during the day or at nighttime.

⛭ Change the vacuum cleaner bag to improve efficiency. It saves electric energy—and human energy too.

⛭ Install storm windows and doors.

⛭ Check with your electric company to see if they offer discounts for "banding" your air conditioner. We save $150 a month by agreeing to have a device on our unit that allows the power company to periodically turn it off if there is an energy shortage in a different part of the state. In the three years we've had the band, we've never noticed the difference, other than the credit on our electric bill!

⛭ If you're not using something, turn it off. When you leave a room, flip off the light switch. If you aren't using an appliance (a hair dryer, for instance, or your coffee maker), unplug it.

⛭ Buy Energy Star–rated dishwashers and hot water heaters. Save up to 25 percent in water costs.

⛭ Set your water heater thermostat to a moderate setting of around 120 degrees Fahrenheit. This keeps the water hot enough to wash clothes but cool enough to prevent badly scalding little hands.

⛭ Wrap the water heater with an insulation kit. This keeps the hot water at its higher temperature while using less energy. You can purchase one from Home Depot or at any home improvement store.

⛭ Periodically drain the water heater from the bottom to remove sediment and allow for more efficient operation.

⛭ To save water and electricity, use your dishwasher, clothes washer, and dryer only when full.

🔢 If you're going to be away from your home for more than three days, turn off the water heater.

🔢 Water your lawn in the early morning hours and only once a week (if possible).

🔢 Make sure attic insulation is at least six inches deep. Save 10 percent on heating and cooling.

Did You Know?

One of the most important—and easy!—things you can do is read your utility bills each month and check the meters for accuracy. Too many people pay their bills without scrutinizing them to make sure they're paying the correct amount. Don't be one of those people!

ROOM BY ROOM

One reason the average American family is not recession-proof is because they live a consumptive lifestyle, especially at home. So let's take a room-by-room tour of your home and see how much we can save. Save $1,185 room by room.

Kitchen

🔢 Combine oven dishes. Select menu items that will cook at the same temperature rather than heating the oven twice at two different temps. Bake as many dishes at once as possible. Save $125 in energy costs.

🔢 Use cloth napkins and real plates. Yes, it's less convenient. But it's cheaper to wash than to buy paper. Save $95 per year.

- Use quality paper products. Sometimes the cheaper versions of paper products end up costing you far more. The Bounty paper towels I use are 25 percent thicker and clothlike, making it easier to handle my cleaning needs. I use half as many sheets because I just rinse, wring, and reopen to get tougher jobs done—this saves me money in the long run. Save $50 per year.
- Maintain your refrigerator. Check seals on your refrigerator and clean the coils. Save $50 per year on energy costs.
- Use slow cookers and pressure cookers instead of the oven.
- Stop the dishwasher after the wash cycle or use the economy cycle. The warmth from the wash cycle will dry the dishes.

Family Room
- Practice a cover-up. If you still have young children at home, you may want to wait to have your furniture recovered. Purchase a quality slipcover for $65 instead of buying a new sofa for $850. Save $785. Place a crocheted doily for $15 on the coffee table to cover scratches made by a speeding Corvette (Hot Wheels size!) instead of purchasing a new table for $130. Save $115.
- Catch it quickly! The best way to make sure oopsies on the carpet and furniture don't stain is to attack them as soon as they occur. You may want to alert the baby-sitter as well! Keep carpet and upholstery cleaner nearby to save on the need to have anything professionally cleaned. Save $95.

Baby's Room

⌖ Make your own baby wipes. I did this for our five
youngest children until they were well into their
toddler years. Here's the recipe:

> 1 round plastic container with lid (about 6
>   inches tall and wide enough to accom-
>   modate a half roll of paper towels)
> 1 roll Bounty heavy-duty paper towels
>   (no cheap store brands)
> 4 tablespoons baby oil
> 4 tablespoons baby shampoo
> 4 tablespoons baby bath
> 1 to 2 cups water (depending on the
>   absorbency of the towels)

Cut a small X (about an inch long) in the plastic
lid of the container. Cut the paper towels in half to
make two short rolls of towels (use one and save
one). Put the three liquid ingredients in the bottom
of the container and add one cup of water. Stir well.
Place the paper towel, cut side up, in the water for a
few minutes. Then turn it over, cut side down, to let
the other side absorb the liquid. Let it sit for five
minutes.

If the roll of paper towels still has dry portions
on it, add more water, ½ cup at a time, at five-
minute intervals, until towels are completely damp
(not dripping, just damp).

After the cardboard center of the paper towel
tube is wet, gently pull it out of the center of the
towels. Pull the towels from the center and thread
through the X in the lid of the plastic container.

Seal. This will keep fresh for up to one month. Save $140 per year, per baby.

Bathrooms

- Fill a quart-size plastic milk or juice bottle with water. Put it in your toilet tank. This fills up space, and you use less water every time you flush. Some people use bricks in their toilet tanks to displace water—but bricks can erode and clog your pipes. Save $150 per year.
- Fix leaky toilets and faucets, especially hot water faucets. One leaky faucet wastes more than 1,300 gallons per year.
- Take a shower instead of a bath. This can save as much as 50 percent of the total hot water used in your home.
- Buy a water-restricted showerhead to give plenty of water and little waste.
- Coordinate baths to conserve hot water. It takes 10 percent of the hot water in the tank to heat the lines to the bathroom. Run the herd in and out of the shower and bath in the same hour.
- Buy the same color towels to save big bucks every year. If you choose white towels, you won't have to buy a new set if one is stained or mildewed. Save $55 per year.
- Fix broken tiles and chipped grout in the bathroom immediately in order to minimize water damage to tiles and the wallboard. The average replacement after major damage costs $350 compared to a $30 repair. Save $320.

Bedrooms

⛭ Just like the towels in the bathroom, buy the same color linens. If you choose all white sheets, you'll only have to buy a top sheet or a fitted sheet if one is torn or damaged. Save $85 per year.

Office (Phone Savings)

⛭ Check to see if there's a toll-free number for the long-distance call you'll make by dialing the toll-free operator at 1-800-555-1212.

⛭ Check with your phone service provider to see if unlimited long-distance calling is available for your plan.

⛭ Don't call directory assistance. You'll pay for the call. Instead, call 1-800-Free-411 (1-800-373-3411). You'll have to listen to a brief advertisement, but you'll get the number you need. Just make sure you have a pen handy; this service will not direct connect you.

⛭ Dial direct whenever possible; don't ask an operator for assistance—unless you *want* to pay a bundle for the call.

⛭ Ask your operator for credit on wrong numbers and disconnects or dropped calls.

⛭ Choose a long-distance carrier that bills in six-second increments so you aren't charged for full minutes when you only use a fraction of a minute.

⛭ Prepaid calling cards are less expensive if you buy the three-cent-per-minute option that many warehouse clubs sell.

⛭ Check your bill carefully; get credit for calls you didn't make.

⚄ Evaluate your need for a cell phone—especially one that has all the bells and whistles.

⚄ Use cell phones for emergencies only and for long distance if those minutes are free in your plan.

⚄ If you're not satisfied with your cell phone service, don't go into the provider's store, instead make a phone call! Ask to speak to cancellations and you will automatically bypass customer service and be connected with a specialist who wants to keep your business and knows all the codes, deals, and special plans you can be put on in order to retain you as a customer. These are deals that are *not* usually available in your cell phone provider's physical store but must be acquired by calling the company.

⚄ Use your phone book or Google. Directory assistance is no longer a free call and can cost up to $2 per request, depending on the service you use.

⚄ Another option instead of calling 411: 1-800-Good-411. This is Google's voice-activated information source that uses easy prompts and contains mainly commercial listings.

⚄ Try Skype. Go to www.skype.com and set up an Internet account so you can talk to your loved ones abroad for only pennies per minute. We use this with our daughter and grandchildren who live in Israel. Skype accepts all major credit cards, and you can load your account with the currency of your choice.

   TIP: If you accidentally load with euros, don't convert to U.S. dollars in the middle of the plan. Instead, use up all your euros, then charge the new amount in dollars. This will save you the conversion costs.

We've got a webcam and so does our family in Israel, so our grandbabies see us and remember who we are, and we can watch them as they grow and hear the new words they are saying (in both English and Hebrew).

Laundry Room

- Use the "manual dryer" outside: a clothesline.
- Use cold water for your laundry. Today's laundry detergents will clean your lightly soiled clothing easily without hot water.
- Try using less laundry detergent. Depending on the water hardness in your area, you might need only half the amount you're currently using. The same applies to your dishwasher.
- Use the partial-load water level adjustment on your clothes washer to customize the water to your current need. If you have a full load of dirty clothes, use the highest water level. If you have a small load, then select your washer's lowest water level.

HOME SAVINGS

- Pay extra on your mortgage principal. If you pay your monthly mortgage *plus* the principal on the next month's payment, and continue to do this, you will find that your mortgage can be paid off in about half the time. Look at the original mortgage loan and see how little of your initial payment goes toward the principal. You are mainly servicing the interest.

But if you make the monthly payment and pay the principal for the next month, and do this every month, it will only increase your payments slightly (depending on your mortgage payment). All of those additional dollars go directly to the principal. This allows you to pay down the principal rapidly, and with proper planning you could end up paying off a thirty-year mortgage in only fifteen years!

⌖ Refinance a $200,000 home at a fixed (not variable) interest rate 1.5 percent lower than your existing loan and minimize your closing costs: save $22,123 over the course of a thirty-year loan, or $737 per year.

If you go from a mortgage rate of 9.28 percent to 5.48 percent, you can save $4,644 per year as your payments go from $1,238 to $851 a month. For a great calculator that can help you crunch your own mortgage refinance numbers, go to the Tool Center at www.elliekay.com.

⌖ *Don't* refinance if you're planning to move within the next three years. If you crunch the numbers of associated closing costs—including points, fees, and other expenses—it seems to take about two to three years to recover those costs and break even.

Did You Know?

Overcharges for mortgage fees are more common than ever. A new study finds that dubious fees may mean consumers are overpaying to get a mortgage, according to data collected from more than ten thousand recent borrowers by the National Mortgage Complaint Center, a watchdog organization that helps consumers avoid overcharges.

Here are the most common mortgage overages and how to avoid them:

- **Inflated Credit Report and Courier Fees**

    Some lenders are charging up to $65 for pulling your credit report. That is unusually high, considering the fact that credit reporting bureaus only charge $6 to $18 per report. Using the same tactics, some lenders charge courier fees for shipping your closing documents for as much as $100, while the majority of overnight express services only charge $22. Tell your lender, up front, that you refuse to pay any more than the going rate for these services.

- **Document Prep and Administration Fees**

    The origination fee should include these services, so don't pay them! Ask your lender to waive these fees.

- **Yield Spread Premiums**

    Lenders increase your interest rate slightly to include origination and other fees so you don't have to pay them out of pocket at closing, but some lenders and mortgage brokers are double-dipping by charging both the fees and the higher interest rate.

    While you are still in the shopping phase for a mortgage provider, ask your broker directly if his firm charges you a "yield spread premium"; if so, confirm with the firm in writing that you shouldn't pay any additional fees. If you define these terms up front, you shouldn't run into the later problem of duplicate fees. If a broker indicates that you will be charged both the yield spread premium and origination and other fees, let her know that is an unacceptable offer and you are going to shop around for a lender who won't charge double fees. With the current squeeze on mortgage providers, real estate has become more of a buyers' market. And if you have a fairly good FICO (credit) score, then you are in the driver's seat to be able to ask for equitable provisions to your loan, which will allow you to keep more of your money at closing time.

- **Padded Title Insurance Fees**

    When you are shopping for lenders, look for all the above, plus look out for those lenders that don't tack on a lot of extra charges for services such as title search and document preparation. These can add hundreds of dollars to your closing costs, and they really should be included in the price of title insurance, which, depending on where you live, can be as high as $6,000.

Insurance

- On your homeowner's insurance, be sure to insure the value of the house itself and *not* the dirt it's on. Save $250 per year.
- Review your policy annually. The first thing to keep in mind is that most people have their homeowner's insurance paid as part of the mortgage payment and don't think to get an annual review of this policy. Every year, you should ask your agent how to reduce costs through discounts for nonsmokers, fire-prevention devices, security systems, or a new tile roof. Most families should carry replacement value on their homes and only up to 90 percent of the property value—*don't* include the land in this coverage. You can't collect more than the home's value if

there is a total loss, so don't pay the additional premiums. Further reduce premiums by increasing the deductible to $500, $1,000, or 1 to 2 percent of the total amount of coverage.

⚏ Make sure you have *replacement value* on personal property insurance. It costs only a little more, and the additional coverage is worthwhile. For example, if the pipes freeze and permanently damage the carpet, replacement value will reimburse the cost of replacing it with the same quality carpet—less the deductible. If you don't carry replacement value, the carpet will be depreciated, which won't leave much of a check to cover the damages.

⚏ When you evaluate your policy, consider adding a Personal Articles Rider/Floater for replacement value on any precious items. If a thief steals jewelry, guns, computer equipment, antiques, coin collections, and other personal items, your homeowner's insurance could cover as little as $500 unless these things are *itemized.* The cost of this additional coverage depends on the total amount of the rider. When the average value of a woman's jewelry in America is estimated at $5,600, this tip could save you more than $5,000 if a thief decides to pay your house a visit while you're at the movies.

TAXES

⚏ Review your real estate taxes—especially now that real estate has taken a dip. I recently spoke with our local county tax assessor, and he said that very few people dispute their tax assessment. But reviewing has its ad-

Did You Know?

You can save a lot on your homeowner's insurance by getting a new quote at renewal time each year. To get started, go to www.freeinsurancequotes.com or www.insweb.com.

vantages. Be aware, though, that unless your situation is an obvious oversight that the assessor agrees with, you will need to be prepared to back up your claim regarding your property value. This could include an appraisal or a comparative market analysis. The comparative market analysis will document recorded sales of houses similar to yours, and these services are sometimes offered free from real estate agents. The assessment by a real estate agent, of course, is not the legal document provided by a licensed appraiser. Also beware of spam or junk mail you receive that comes from a tax reassessment service—they are selling, not buying or simply providing free info!

▨ Keep a list of all improvements on your home—from a new air conditioner to a water heater. You should check with your tax advisor each year, but the IRS usually defines improvements as those items that "add to the value of your home, prolong its useful life, or adapt it to new uses." Examples include putting a recreation room in your unfinished basement, adding another bathroom or bedroom, putting up a fence, installing new plumbing or wiring, getting a new roof, or paving your driveway. Videotape all these improvements and keep the tape in a safe place.

Question:

Rather than paying the huge interest rates on credit cards, would it be better to take out a home equity loan or a HELOC credit card and pay my debts?

Answer:

A home equity line of credit (HELOC) is similar to your banker selling you a gun and teaching you how to pull the trigger to shoot yourself in the foot. That's what happens when you secure a HELOC credit card. The credit companies tout it as "a convenient way to access your home's equity without refinancing your mortgage every time you need money." Yeah, right.

If you're truly hard up for cash and faced with the awful choice of paying for daily expenses such as gas, groceries, and utility bills by credit card or by using a HELOC, you could argue that a HELOC is the better option because it's the least expensive in the short term. That's because HELOCs, which are tied to the prime rate, carry lower rates than credit cards, and the interest is typically tax deductible. The problem is that it becomes too easy to keep using it for gas, groceries, and utility bills.

Unless you're unemployed or on the verge of losing your car or home, avoid a HELOC credit card. It's just another way to borrow on your future in order to live for today. It's also another way to incur more debt, and it will keep you from paying off your home that much sooner. This practice is what made a lot of families go "under water" in their mortgages during the housing downturn in recent years—which means they owe more than their house is worth because a HELOC is tying up their equity.

Question:

My husband just returned from deployment in Iraq. Now that he's back, we'd like to buy a home. Are there any special loans for the military that will help us save money?

Answer:

Consider getting a VA loan. According to data from the Department of Veterans Affairs, less than 10 percent of the 23.8 million U.S. veterans (2.1 million) have VA loans. Daniel Chookaszian, vice president of veteran lending at American Street Mortgage Company, who specializes in VA loans, says, "VA loans have looser underwriting standards than conventional and even Federal Housing Administration (FHA) loans. With a VA loan, veterans can get 100 percent financing without private mortgage insurance (PMI) and interest rates around 5 percent." The other advantage is that sellers are allowed to cover all closing costs, prepaid items, and discounts. This lets borrowers essentially walk into their new home with no down payment, no closing costs, and a thirty-year fixed rate of around 5 percent with no mortgage insurance. In the present market, for veterans who cannot put down 20 percent toward their home purchase, a better loan just doesn't exist.

To qualify for a VA loan, you have to have an automated certificate of eligibility (ACE), which you can apply for at https://vip.vba.va.gov/portal/VBAH/Home. This form specifies the veteran's eligibility, which is determined by three factors: (a) whether the veteran was honorably discharged; (b) whether the veteran has used eligibility in the past; (c) whether the VA is still guaranteeing a previous loan for the veteran.

Veterans must also provide proof of their honorable military status. If you have used some of your VA eligibility in the past, and if that loan was assumed by another veteran, then you would deduct the amount outstanding on that loan from total lifetime eligibility.

In 2008, there was a 150 percent increase in VA loan guarantees, which experts expect will continue into 2010. This increase has proven the VA loan's ability to weather the storm of the current housing crisis. The VA has always offered safe, strong loans, and never serviced subprime, stated, or "no doc" borrowers. The VA is still guaranteeing the 25 percent down payment for veterans on purchases and refinances—something that 18 million veterans have participated in since 1944. There's also help for veterans to obtain cash-out refinances up to 100 percent, if they got themselves into subprime adjustable rate mortgages or if their home value has dropped due to market conditions. It's important to go to someone who specializes in VA loans, such as Daniel Chookaszian at daniel@americanstreet.com. It's not a benefit if you don't take advantage of it!

Question:

I'm a renter, but everyone tells me I should buy a home. What are some things I should do or look out for as I apply for a mortgage?

Answer:

Good for you! You're right. Purchasing something can be the best option—because after paying those monthly payments, you have something in your name to show for it. Here are a few dos and don'ts to strengthen your position with a lender.

DO make on-time debt payments. Every thirty-, sixty-, or ninety-day delinquency on a loan or credit card will reduce your credit score. If it appears that you have trouble making debt payments on time, a lender will be hesitant to loan you money.

DO choose carefully which payment you're going to miss if you must miss a payment. If you can't pay a bill for a few months for some reason (such as if you lost your job), be strategic in choosing that missed payment. Miss a credit card payment first, followed by the payment on any installment loan you might have (such as a car loan), and *finally* an existing mortgage payment. A missed mortgage payment will have the greatest impact on your credit score and will also impact your ability to get a good home loan in the future. A missed credit card payment will not have as great an impact as a missed car payment.

DO pay off debt. Pay off as many smaller debts as you can so you'll have a better chance of getting a good mortgage rate. Even if you end up putting down a smaller amount at closing and have a larger mortgage, you'll be better off than the high interest rates of most consumer debt.

DO know how much house you can afford before you talk with a mortgage broker. Check out the calculators on my Web site at www.elliekay.com to see what you can comfortably and reasonably afford.

DON'T make big purchases before you apply for a mortgage. If you have to get a loan for a large purchase, such as a $15,000 auto loan, it could prevent you from qualifying for the mortgage amount you want. Don't do this before you request a mortgage loan. Lenders do not look favorably at adding debt on top of debt. When you secure your mortgage loan before you buy a new car or furniture, you've maximized your credit rating while it is at its highest number, and this will add up to a lower interest rate and a lower monthly house payment.

DON'T live beyond your means. If you try to obtain a loan that would raise your payments from $500 in rent to a whopping $1,600 per month for principal, interest, and insurance, then you are likely to experience what the industry calls "payment shock." You don't want to live beyond your means. A lender will look at this differential, and you will find yourself in one of two situations: (1) you won't qualify for the loan, or (2) you will end up having to cover too much loan with too little money.

DO get preapproved rather than prequalified. When you are *prequalified* for a loan, you are given an estimate of how much you will qualify for after you've submitted income, credit, and debt information. In this case, the lender does not pull credit reports, check debt-to-income ratios, or perform other underwriting steps. But by getting *preapproved*, these latter steps are performed, and you are that much closer to obtaining a loan and locking in a rate and term. The first is an estimate; the latter is much closer to the final product.

DO decide up-front what type of mortgage you can handle. Everyone has a money personality—some are born spenders and others are born savers. It's important to know your money personality when it comes to getting a mortgage. If you take out a thirty-year fixed-rate loan rather than a fifteen-year mortgage and invest the money saved on monthly payments, you might earn a higher return on your money in the long run. But few money personalities have this kind of discipline. If you're the kind of person who spends any extra money you have, it would be better to get the shorter term, which will force you to invest your money toward paying off your house in a shorter amount of time. Just make sure you can afford the higher payment on the shorter loan.

DO remember the hidden extra costs to home ownership. You will have to cover short-term and long-term repairs and maintenance and property taxes.

3

Save Big on Transportation

12-Minute Tip #2: Instead of buying a new car, buy one that is a year old but still has a warranty left on it to save an average of $5,000 per car. Take 12 minutes to do a history search on your potential used-car purchase by spending $25 to $40 at either www.carfax.com or www.autocheck.com. This time investment can save you at least $1,200 that you would otherwise spend if you bought a lemon!

I learned at an early age that buying used is oftentimes buying best when it comes to cars—and many other goods. In 1978, I purchased a Datsun B210 for $950, and I drove it four years. I saved my paycheck from a part-time job and baby-sitting so I could pay cash. And from the time I was sixteen, I also paid for the gas, insurance, and maintenance on my car. Oh, how I wish I could still pay the price per gallon from back then!

Do you remember the good old days when gasoline was 99 cents a gallon? Nowadays—if you're like me, and most every other person in America—you cringe every time you drive past a gas station. You almost feel like you have to take out a second mortgage just to get to work! (I don't recommend that, by the way.)

For better or worse, though, we are dependent on our automobiles. We live in a commuter society where 90 percent of us drive. Most of us drive an average of 12,000 miles per year and report that we're behind the wheel for an average of 87 minutes a day. And for parents with children at home, your average jumps to 104 minutes (compared to people without kids at home at 77 minutes).[1] In fact, when my youngest five were all home and involved in two activities a piece for a total of ten different interests each week, I felt like I was in the car 24/7. But that *might* be a wee bit of an exaggeration.

If you commute to work, which most of us do, look at these average drive times:

Commute time: 26 minutes

On a good day: 19 minutes

On a bad day: 46 minutes[2]

We happen to live in California where Interstate 405 was recently pronounced the busiest highway in the world. So here's my commute time to Los Angeles International Airport to catch a flight:

Commute time: 2.5 hours

On a good day: there are no good days on the 405

On a bad day: 6 hours and I miss my flight

Traffic congestion adds at least a half-hour per day to a worker's drive, fifteen minutes each way. Hello! That's a lot of time and potential money.

But it's not just about time. Remember that time is money. And not just gas money. Gas is only a portion of what it costs to drive. As you look at how much you have to spend each month on transportation costs, you have to consider the hidden costs as well: car payments; interest included in car payments; upkeep, including oil changes, tires, tire rotations, tune-ups; insurance; registration; license renewals; parking; tolls; and car washes. And don't forget road construction costs. As my friends who live in Chicago can attest, winter driving brings potholes that can mess up your car's alignment.

Before we look at how much money you can save on transportation costs, it's important to figure out how much you're already spending in this area. To make it easier, go to my Web site, www.elliekay.com, click on the Tool Center, and use the Car Operating Cost Calculator.

As I discuss in my book *Living Rich for Less,* after housing and utilities, transportation is your next largest category of spending. You should be spending no more than 15 percent of your take-home income on transportation. Too many of us are spending way more than that, though!

If you live in an area where you can carpool or take public transportation, that not only saves money, it saves the earth as well. Unfortunately, that doesn't apply to the vast majority of those reading this book. So other than chucking your car (yeah, right), here are some ways to really save (as much as 25 percent or $750 per car per year!) on your transportation costs.

❧

GAS

▤ Gas prices can vary by as much as 20 cents per gallon between stations less than a mile apart. Who can explain? So before you decide simply to pull into the closest station, go to Web sites such as www.gasprice watch.com to find the cheapest price for gas both at home and en route. Depending on current gas prices, you could save $5 or more on each twenty-gallon fill-up.

🔲 Pace your driving. Jackrabbit starts and constant speeding up and slowing down cost precious gas mileage. Seriously, is it *really* that important to speed around a slow driver so you can stop at a red light three seconds before the other guy? Pace yourself—you'll save money and stress, and you really won't have that much of a time difference. Instead, put on some "spa music" and take deep breaths—yes, I'm smiling as I say this especially when I think about driving the 405 on the way to LAX.

🔲 No speeding! Speeding will only speed up your fuel consumption. According to the Department of Energy (DOE), it takes a lot of energy for your vehicle to push the air out of the way as you speed down the road. Driving the speed limit of 65 versus 75 can save as much as 15 percent on fuel consumption because of the energy needed for higher speeds.

🔲 Have you ever driven behind someone who constantly taps his brakes? Tap…tap…tap. And the brake lights go *blink, blink, blink*. It can make you crazy! Put on your spa music and relax. Try to keep plenty of space between your car and the car ahead of you so you can coast to slow down if you need to rather than tapping the brakes and accelerator. A good rule of thumb for how much distance to keep is to practice the three-second rule: as the car ahead of you passes a fixed object such as a sign or light pole, count to three before you pass it. Smooth drivers waste less fuel, which means they save more money! And they can save up to 10 percent on their gas mileage.

⛬ Good news for those of you who, like me, enjoy riding with the air conditioning. Now you have no reason to feel guilty that you aren't getting fresh air. At speeds of 40 miles per hour or greater, it costs more to leave the windows open (due to drag) than it does to run the air conditioning. In our California town the summer temps reach 110 degrees, so this savings tip makes me especially happy, plus it saves my hair from getting messed up by the wind!

⛬ Pitch the junk! According to www.fueleconomy.gov, for every extra hundred pounds you carry around in your car, your gas mileage declines by 2 percent. So take your golf clubs, soccer chairs, tool boxes, Salvation Army book donations, and all the other *junk* out of your *trunk*. Otherwise you're paying more to haul it around because the added weight means you have to use more gas to get your car going. Cleaning out your car is a great way to lose weight and the easiest diet you'll ever go on!

⛬ While we're on the subject of getting rid of excess weight. In California I don't have to deal with this, but if you live in an area that gets snow and ice you do. One of the easiest ways to save gas mileage and money is to make sure you clear the snow and ice off your car completely before you drive it. It's not enough just to clear the car's windows. Everything needs to come off the entire car. Remember that a hundred pounds can reduce your mileage, and ice and especially wet snow can add up to a hundred pounds quicker than I can say, "Money doesn't grow on snowmen!"

⌘ *Still* speaking of ditching the weight…lose that fifteen pounds you've been putting off losing. You'll save 5 mpg per month! Hey, as a mom of seven, this is a case where I should be taking my own advice!

⌘ Pressurize and maintain. Make sure you have the correct air pressure in your tires (for the correct amount, check the owner's manual—you know, that booklet you received when you bought the car that you dumped in the glove box and haven't looked at since), change the air filters regularly, and maintain your vehicle with regular tune-ups. Save 5 percent per year on gas.

⌘ Check your gas cap's gasket. Believe it or not, if the gas cap doesn't properly fit and seal, then gas vapors will escape from the car. If the gasket looks old and cracked, get a new gasket from an auto parts store or from Wal-Mart's auto department.

⌘ Premium, schemium. According to AAA, only 5 percent of vehicles in the U.S. require premium gas—it does not help your vehicle to pay more for it. Buy the regular stuff and have no worries.

⌘ Try using your legs. If your work commute is twenty-one miles each way, then biking or walking may not be the best option (unless you really *want* to get up at midnight to leave for your daytime work shift). But walking or biking could be an option for closer commutes, such as running errands. You'll get some exercise, de-stress, and enjoy the great outdoors and the extra cash that will end up in your pocket.

- When gas skyrocketed to almost $5 a gallon, several people I know purchased good, used motorcycles (and helmets). If you're not a daredevil or if you are one of my children, then I don't recommend this option, since motorcycles take a special license and are more dangerous on the road because they can be missed more easily by drivers who aren't paying attention. But scooters and motorcycles do get better gas mileage (scooters can get 80 mpg and motorcycles can get 55 mpg) than most vehicles (which get 30 mpg) and can save you money.

- Car- or vanpooling can be an option for a work commute. If you're like one of my friends, she likes to drive alone because it allows her to unwind after a long day at work. But once a week, she joins the carpool group and saves money that day by letting someone else do the driving.

- Combine errands. Instead of running errands several days a week, combine and run all of them on the same day to save time and money.

CAR SALES

- Drive the car you have now for a while longer. The least expensive car you can own is usually the "paid for" car you're driving right now. Before you look to buy another car, ask yourself, "Why am I buying it?" Are you tired of your present car? Can your car be repaired without major expense? How many miles do you have left on your present car?

🕮 Consider purchasing a late-model, low-mileage, mechanically sound, well-maintained used car. Take the car to a reliable mechanic and pay him to look it over. If at all possible, try to talk to the previous owner of the car before you buy it. Be leery of re-painted portions of the car—it usually indicates an accident. Look carefully under the car for rust. Avoid buying a car from anyone who smokes. Cigarette smoke damages seals, glue, and upholstery.

🕮 Don't buy a lemon. You might be told that the used Mercedes 280SLK Roadster that you want to buy was only driven by a little grandma to and from the grocery store. By ordering a complete vehicle check at www.carfax.com or www.autocheck.com, you can get a complete history on your potential purchase (as mentioned in 12-Minute Tip #2). This includes a title history (how many owners), whether the vehicle has been in accidents, whether the car is a lemon, the true mileage, etc. This little tip can save you thousands of dollars in repair costs and keep you from buying a bad car.

🕮 Try to sell your car privately rather than trade it in. If you trade in your vehicle to a car dealership, you'll get significantly less for it. It doesn't matter how much the salesman says he's giving you for the trade. Salespeople often inflate the value of trade-ins and then figure the inflated amount in the negotiated price on the vehicle you purchase. Detail your car yourself—washing and waxing it to a glorious shine.

As you clean and scrub, think of all the extra money you'll make with this minimum effort—you may be able to get $1,000 to $2,000 more for your vehicle!

⊞ If you *must* buy new, avoid buying the newest, latest, greatest model as soon as it comes out. Instead, buy an end-of-the-year clearance model, a demonstrator model, or a rental car. December and January are the best times to get these bargains because that's when dealerships experience their lowest annual sales. Buy a cheaper model of the same vehicle rather than the luxury model. Buy the smallest car that will still fit your needs. Be prepared with realistic prices by doing your research on the value of the car at either www.kbb.com or www.edmunds.com. Print out these values and walk into the dealership armed with the facts.

Did You Know?

The average depreciation of a new car during the first year can be up to 31 percent of the price you paid for it. Incredible! With most new cars, you lose $6,000 as soon as you drive it off the car lot. Let someone else own it for that expensive year!

INSURANCE

⊞ Your mama said you should drive the speed limit, and insurance companies agree. Each ticket and each accident add surcharge points and additional premiums to the cost of a policy. So if you feel you were given a ticket unfairly, it pays to fight it. If another person was at fault in an accident, call the police to the scene to file a report that proves no fault and removes any surcharge points on your policy. Go for higher deductibles on comprehensive and collision in order to insure big accidents, not fender benders.

⊞ If you are in an accident that isn't your fault and you and the other driver have the same insurance company, do not allow the insurance company to use your policy to pay for the damages to you and your car. If you do, regardless of the fact that the accident wasn't your fault, guess whose insurance rates will go up? Make sure the entire accident goes on the other person's insurance policy. But that's *only* if you aren't at fault!

⊞ Compare and beware. Secure estimates from at least three major companies before purchasing automobile insurance. Many people I talk with feel helpless when it comes to car insurance—they don't understand the lingo, don't know where or how to shop around to compare rates, and don't think they have much control over how much they pay for coverage. But, today, shopping for car insurance is easier than it's ever been.

Lots of help is available online, in person, or by phone.

For example, Progressive Insurance has customer service reps available 24/7 to help people get a quote and buy over the phone. They have more than thirty thousand independent agents all over the country for people who prefer in-person counsel. And their site—www.progressive.com—lets people get a quote and compare its direct rate with rates from other companies. And people can even name their price for car insurance—when they get a quote for a policy, they can tell Progressive how much they want to pay and then see the closest available package of coverages, limits, and deductibles offered based on the price they've entered. This is the perfect solution for everyone's budget.

Rates for car insurance differ from company to company. They can even vary depending on *how* you buy—companies that sell both directly by phone or online and through agents often have different rates. And it's important to note that rates from one method of buying aren't always lower than the other.

So shopping can almost certainly lead to savings, but according to a recent survey, more than a third of U.S. drivers never shop for car insurance! Companies like Progressive make shopping easy, can provide you with helpful information, and can answer your questions. And best of all, because they sell online, by phone, and through local agents, you can choose how you'd like to do business with them.

✂ Reduce the cost of car insurance by buying the right kind of car. Some vehicles are far more expensive to insure than others, so check with an insurance agent before buying. If possible, use the least expensive car to travel to and from work. "For pleasure only" is the rating used for SAHM (stay-at-home moms), and it

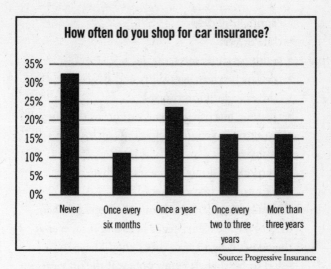

How often do you shop for car insurance?

Source: Progressive Insurance

is one of the least expensive ratings, so use that on the most expensive vehicle.

Take every discount possible. The following discounts depend on your insurance company as well as your individual state's regulations. So you might not get all of these discounts, but it's worth asking the question. For the average two-car family with a teenage driver, for example, combine a homeowner's and auto policy, be a nonsmoker and a good student, install a car alarm system, store the vehicle in a garage versus carport or on the street, ask how your policy is rated, and see what discounts exist for drivers with a safety course certificate. Save $900 per year.

Ask your company about the following discounts:

- nonsmokers
- nondrinkers (total abstainers)

- antitheft devices
- safe drivers
- multicar discounts
- drivers between ages thirty and sixty
- driver's education courses
- parking in a garage versus carport or the street
- working in certain professions, such as the military
- carrying multiple policies with them, such as auto and homeowner's

⛭ Carefully consider when your teenagers get their driver's license. Once teens have a license, even if they don't have a car to drive, they'll have to be listed somewhere on your policy. If the only cars on the policy are fully covered vehicles (comprehensive and collision), this addition could double your premiums!

The best option is to put a teenager as the principal driver on an older vehicle that only carries the basic package—liability, medical, and uninsured motorists. Consider letting the teen pay a portion (or all) of his insurance premium. In our family we will pay the insurance until the teen gets a ticket or is involved in an accident (whether they are at fault or not), then she has to pay her own insurance. It's an extra incentive to drive safely.

NOTE: Insurance policies vary by state. Ask your insurance agent to clarify all discounts, penalties, and possible variables (such as driver assignments). The better informed you are, the wiser your money-saving choices can be.

OTHER SAVINGS

⬚ Many states that have toll roads also provide an electronic pass (I-Pass, Easy-Pass, etc.). They save time, but also can save you money on tolls. In Illinois, for instance, drivers are penalized for not having the pass by being charged double. The good news is that many states share those passes. So you can use an Illinois pass in Indiana and several other states.

⬚ Use discounts and coupons for local garages. Go to my Web site at www.elliekay.com and click on www.valpak.com or www.hotcoupons.com for a list of the garages in your area that offer these special savings.

⬚ Take advantage of frequent buyer programs. Some shops offer one free oil change when you buy ten. Often you can even use coupons on the oil changes you purchase.

Did You Know?

Many cities are now posting cameras at intersections to catch drivers who run red lights or fail to stop completely before making right-hand turns, and in some places, even to nail speeders. They video the vehicle's license plate and catalog the traffic violation, and send a handy-dandy ticket through the mail, which cannot be contested in traffic court. Obey the traffic laws and save hundreds every year.

❧

Question:

I've heard friends talk about how much better leasing is than buying, since a car depreciates as soon as you drive it off the lot. Plus leasing allows you a new car every several years. What do you think? Is leasing better than owning?

Answer:

The only way to spend more on a car than buying it new is to lease one. Leasing a car is the most expensive means of driving. The only exceptions are if you use it for business, anticipate extremely high mileage, or there is a substantial tax savings. If the only way you can drive the car you want is to lease it, then pass on it. There's a less expensive car for you that will still meet your needs.

Question:

If you get a speeding ticket and they offer to remove it from your record by taking a driver's safety course, is it worth it since you usually have to pay for the class?

Answer:

I do believe that it *is* worth taking the course to remove the ticket from your record. Even one ticket can add surcharge points to your auto insurance policy, making it more expensive. Plus, when you turn that driver's safety course certificate in to your auto insurance company, you can get as much as an additional 15 percent off your policy!

Question:

We have three teenagers who will be driving soon, and our local driving school charges around $350 per child! Is there a way to save money on driving school?

Answer:

There are a number of ways to save money on driving school. First, see if your local public school district offers a summer course. Second, you can negotiate the price for the school. I was able to get $50 off just by telling the school I was shopping around with their competitors. Third, you can look into the online versions of this school. Just Google "driving school online in [type your state here]." Just be sure you check out the school at the Better Business Bureau at www.bbb.org. Some of these courses are as affordable as $19.99, but they also put the driving portion of the work on the parents. So if you're skittish about driving with a newbie, then you might want to splurge for the traditional school.

4

Save Big on Food

12-Minute Tip #3: Take twelve minutes each week to scour sale ads and match up coupons or go to www.couponmom.com, where they do all the work for you! Layer the savings by shopping sales, adding coupon values, double coupons, clipless coupons, store coupons, and/or clearances to save hundreds a month. Save $1,200 a month on food.

Let's talk about food. I love food—and chocolate is my favorite food group! I also love to save money on food. When you have a family the size of mine (I shop for seven), you have to learn to spend frugally or you end up in the poor house. How much have I saved our family? I'm glad you asked. My *average* receipt has been $120 before coupons and only $50 (or less) after coupons. Our family's grocery budget has been $250 per month, and I often came in under budget. A typical family of seven in the United States (with children the ages of ours) spends $12,218 per year for *food alone*. We included cleaning products, toiletries, and diapers in our annual budget of $3,000. Consequently, according to the national average, I saved our family well over $9,000 every year.

Some of the greatest joy I receive is knowing that I'm feeding my family well, that I'm sharing with others who are in need to help them eat well, and that I'm teaching my children the importance of saving money. In my book *Living Rich for Less,* I tell the story of how my son Jonathan saved a bundle of money on his own at the grocery store when he was *eleven years old.* His bill, had he paid regular price for everything, would have been $28.60. Instead, after he took advantage of his coupons and sales, he spent $1.80. Yes, you read that right. If an eleven-year-old can save that kind of cash…

Every month you should be spending 10 percent of your income on food—and that includes dining out. Nowadays, that seems pretty impossible, especially when you look at how expensive restaurants have become. A family of two can eat modestly at Red Lobster and spend more than $80 after tax and tip. I don't consider that cheap! And some couples eat out every other night. That's a lot of cash sliding out of your grasp. Just imagine what you could do with all that extra cash floating around, eating great food both at home and in restaurants, and not padding the pockets of grocery store and restaurant owners. Here are some ways to get started.

$\sim$

GROCERIES

Before You Leave Home

- Do your homework. Before you leave home, the more prepared you are—armed with information, sales papers, and coupons—the more money you'll save. Just take a look at the ways you can use coupons and sales.

- *Store cards.* Also referred to as "clipless coupons." Sign up for a card at the customer service desk. Then when the cashier scans it at the checkout, you'll receive all the store's special values for the week.

- *Sale ads.* The store's weekly sale ads either come in the mail or are part of the midweek newspaper inserts. Match up the sale ads with some of the other savings factors listed, and you'll soon find yourself with products for pennies.

- *Manufacturer's coupons.* These are the traditional coupons you find in the Sunday paper, in the blinking dispensers in the grocery store aisles, on the products that you can tear off and use immediately, inside the box or packaging that you can use the next time you're at the grocery, or that are issued automatically at the checkout after you've purchased your groceries.

- *Double coupons.* Some stores offer double coupons, where the manufacturer's coupon is worth twice the face value—a 50-cent coupon would be worth $1.00. Each store issues limitations, such as "only double up to $1.00," so check the customer service desk for details. Go to the links page at www.elliekay.com to find a link listing all the stores that double coupons in your state.

- *Web bucks.* When you purchase items with coupons good for "cash off your next shopping trip," you will automatically get these invaluable cash-off coupons. When I shopped on the show *Good Morning Texas,* the total before coupons was $127. After coupons, I paid $22 and received $20 in Web bucks that I could use on my next trip—now that's a lot of green!

⌗ Don't use the menu-planning method for shopping. In other words, you decide what you're going to eat for the week, then go to the grocery store and purchase all the ingredients. Instead, plan your menus for the week according to what you already have in your pantry. Since the majority of things I buy are purchased on sale and with a coupon, I know I've paid the lowest price possible for those products in my pantry.

⌗ Don't leave home without a grocery list! It's a known fact among consumer researchers that people who shop with a list (and stick to it) consistently spend as much as 30 percent less. Using a list will not only save you money, it will save you time.

⌗ If possible, shop alone. Leave children and/or your spouse at home. Sans family, your concentration is much better and you're less likely to make quick, costly decisions.

⌗ If you like a particular item, check the package to see if the company has a toll-free customer number. By calling, you can often get coupons for that item. I've received "free" coupons and many cents-off ones too.

Did You Know? _____

Do you love a particular name-brand product but seem never able to find a coupon for it? Go to your favorite brand-name company site to check out available coupons and savings. Or call the toll-free operator at 1-800-555-1212 and ask for the toll-free number of your favorite brand. Then call and ask them to send you coupons. You will then get on their regular mailing list and receive other promotional offers.

In the Store

⌷⌷ Take advantage of unadvertised savings and clearances you can find only by walking the aisles. As much as 50 percent of the week's sales are not advertised.

⌷⌷ Shop the loss leaders. A loss leader is an advertised item (usually the lead-off sale price listed on the front page of the store circular) designed to entice buyers into a store. Often the store will lose money on these products, but they'll make up the difference when Aunt Harriet comes to their store for her weekly shopping. If you have the time, shop the loss leaders at each store and leave the regular-priced stuff for dear Auntie.

⌷⌷ Better yet, shop at stores that honor competitor's ads (this saves gas money, as well). Why shop all over town looking for loss leaders when you don't have to? Many Wal-Mart Superstores, for instance, will honor competitor's ads. All you have to do is take in the competitor's ad with the sale price on any of the items you want. Check with the store manager, but know that they usually substitute other store brands with their own brand. For example, I had an ad for twelve packs of IGA-brand soda in the sale circular I brought to Wal-Mart. The store substituted its Great Value brand for that soda, and I got it for the sale price.

Most stores that offer this additional service do have some restrictions. They will usually not honor advertised store coupons, percentage discounts, club card specials, or buy-one-get-one-free specials. But those guaranteed straight-out matches for the lowest price are great for your time, money, gas, and serenity!

⌘ Use those rain checks! Sometimes I'm grateful when they are out of an item, especially if my coupon has some time on it before it expires. I can usually request a higher quantity on my rain check and have time to collect more coupons for that item while I wait for it to be restocked. I frequently get free items this way.

⌘ Look "high and low" for bargains. Marketing experts depend on impulse buying. They place the most expensive items at eye level and the bargains on the upper and lower shelves. Look high and low for the best deals—and say no to the pricey stuff.

⌘ Just buy a handful. If your recipe only calls for a few pieces of cauliflower or broccoli, don't waste money on an entire head—especially if you or someone in your family is not inclined to eat those items. Pick up what you need from the salad bar or only select a small quantity of that item from the produce section and avoid waste.

🖼 Don't waste money on egg substitutes; make your own by simply using egg whites. Most of these pricey items have primarily egg whites, with dyes and thickeners added.

🖼 Make your own flavored yogurt by purchasing the least expensive yogurt—plain (which incidentally is usually the healthiest)—and mixing it with fresh fruits or preserves.

🖼 Quick-cooking rice can cost twice as much. Buy long-grain rice, cook a greater quantity than you need, and freeze what is left over to use as needed.

🖼 Not all five-pound bags of grapefruit are created equal. They can vary by as much as half a pound, so weigh before you buy.

🖼 Ask your grocer about late-day markdowns in the bakery, meat, dairy, and floral departments. Meats that are near their expiration date can easily be frozen and then used immediately after thawing.

🖼 For meat, buy when it's on sale and stock up. Even if you don't have a large freezer, you can still prioritize and maximize your freezer space by packing items in plastic freezer bags or freezer containers. Then you'll have room for chicken breasts when they go on sale for 79 cents a pound.

🖼 When you purchase meat (that's on sale!) always get the most meat in the weight range they offer. That way, when you prepare it, you can freeze the remaining for another meal or two.

᳓ Consider eating less meat. Buy a bag of beans for 99
   cents, throw them in a slow cooker with some celery,
   onions, potatoes, and carrots. Little work, little clean
   up, great flavor, wonderful health benefits, big savings.
᳓ You don't have to sacrifice by never buying brand-
   name products. Many shoppers I talk to firmly believe they'll save the most money by avoiding
   brand-name purchases. But if you buy items on sale
   and with coupons, this isn't necessarily true, especially when the brand name is a value product. Savvy
   financial planning means choosing everyday items
   that give you more bang for your buck. Did you
   know, for example, that you can save money when
   washing your dishes?

   For example, Dawn Ultra contains 30 percent
   more cleaning ingredients per drop than the leading
   nonconcentrated brand, unlike some larger bottles
   of dish liquid that have more water. With Dawn
   Ultra, you get what you pay for, more power, not
   more water. I especially like a value product like this
   because I can also clean more dishes without the
   water feeling greasy.

   Dawn Direct Foam absorbs 2X more grease
   than regular dishwashing liquids using breakthrough
   product technology and an innovative foaming
   pump—it can clean one sinkful of dishes with just
   one pump! Value products like Dawn may cost a
   bit more initially while shopping, but will save you
   money long term because of its superior grease-
   fighting power over regular dish liquids—which
   means the bottle lasts longer and so does your dollar!

🔁 Don't forget warehouse clubs for big savings. Since those clubs usually sell everything in super-duper, extra-large size, consider shopping there with some friends and splitting the food and costs. (I go into more detail on warehouse clubs and other places to save in *Living Rich for Less.* If you're serious about saving money on food, and you don't already own that book, then check it out from the library or go to my Web site to purchase a copy.)

Did You Know?

Over the course of a lifetime, there may be items where you are overcharged as much as 50 percent. This could add up to a lifetime average of 15 percent overcharges on all purchases overall. So check the checker. As you are checking out anywhere be sure you watch with an eagle eye what you are being charged. If you are overcharged, bring it to the cashier's attention right away. Some stores even have an "It's right or it's free" policy, where if they charge you an incorrect amount, the item is free! I got a $16 double bag of diapers free when a local grocer, who had this guarantee policy, overcharged me.

EATING OUT

🔁 Have you ever *really* stopped to think about how much money you're *giving* away by buying your coffee from places like Starbucks? Ouch. You could just about finance a small country's GNP for a year. Why not make your own coffee and pour it into a travel mug every day? Coffee makers have come a long way, you know. We have a coffeepot with a timer on it: we do the two-minute prep work the night before, set the clock, and our coffee is ready when we wake up. Save $20 or more a week.

- Microwaveable meals are much better than they were even ten years ago. Consider taking those to work for lunch instead of going out for a burger. Save $25 or more a week.

- Buy frozen fruit when it's not in season. This is the least expensive way to have your fruit and eat it too. Because you take only the amount you need from the frozen bag, you don't have to worry about spoilage, and you don't pay out-of-season prices that you pay for fresh.

- Go to your favorite restaurant's Web site by entering www.(favorite restaurant's name).com. For example, go to www.claimjumper.com and see what promotional offers may be posted.

- For offers at your local restaurants, check out www.valpak.com. Or to find bargain restaurants neighborhood by neighborhood go to www .citysearch.com.

- Want to try a new restaurant but don't want to pay full price? Go to www.restaurant.com, a site that issues coupons and gift certificates for more than six thousand eateries around the country. Our family picks a spot and pays $10 for a $25 gift certificate— we save more than 50 percent in the process. The average restaurant bill for a family of four is $86. Using this method, our family saves $43 x 52 weeks = $2,236. Sometimes, these $25 gift certificates are on sale for only $2, and our savings are as much as 80 percent! Not bad, huh?

▨ Do a lunch out instead of a dinner. The average lunch costs anywhere from $3 to $15 less than the average dinner, plus the portions are usually more health friendly. If you want to go to the $50-an-entrée hot spot to celebrate your baby being potty trained, then opt for lunch and save $15 over the price of dinner. Lunching instead of "dinnering" saves an average of $9 per person x 2 (for a couple) = $18 savings per week x 52 weeks = $936 annual savings.

▨ If you eat out frequently (at least once a week), why not get rewards for it? Check out the secure site at www.rewardsnetwork.com and register your credit or debit card to get up to 20 percent of the bill credited to your account when you eat at one of the ten thousand participating restaurants. Be aware that this option requires a $49 annual registration fee. But if you combine this savings with the previous tips, you could save and/or bank up to 70 percent of your restaurant bill! Eating out once a week for a family of four would equal $86/week at 20 percent savings x 52 weeks = $895.

▨ Pay for college by eating out! Go to www.upromise .com and sign up for free membership. Every time you eat out at a participating partner, they will put a percentage of your purchase in a 529 account for your child's college. You can also get grandparents, aunts and uncles, and friends to sign up for this "free" money and put it toward your child's education.

⊞ Check out the rewards programs for your favorite restaurants. Again, this is a great option if you eat there a lot. It's free to sign up (online), and your card gets scanned each time you eat at that restaurant. A friend of mine eats at Qdoba once a week and gets free lunches over and over.

⊞ While the rule of thumb is that you should never pay money for coupons, the local coupon book is the exception. These books, commonly known as Entertainment or Happenings books, are used primarily as fund-raisers for organizations. They include coupons for free or reduced-price meals, services, admissions, and other values. They are usually worth the price you pay for them and usually last for about a year. Go to www.entertainment .com to find a coupon book that is available for 150 metro markets and costs between $25 and $45. Preview the coupon booklet for your area (or an area where you will vacation) to see if the coupons are ones you will use. An added benefit: you'll not only save on eating out, but you can also save on movie theaters, theme parks, dry cleaning, and at local shops. Average advertised total book savings— $17,000. To redeem only 25 percent is an annual savings of $4,250.

⊞ Check the Sunday FSIs (free-standing inserts)—the ones you're using to clip grocery store coupons—for chain restaurant coupons. And the weekday paper may alert you to special days when an eatery offers buy-one-get-one-free meals, kids eat free, or early bird specials. Average FSI savings are 25 percent for a family of four, or a total of $15 per fast-food dinner. This savings x 52 weeks = $780.

✄ The next time you order pizza, ask what the specials or coupon values are for the week. Three out of four pizza shops will give you the coupon value just for asking—even if you don't have the coupons! You can save anywhere from 20 to 50 percent (on a buy-one-get-one-free special).

Did You Know?

Many restaurants are now charging $2 or more for soda, coffee, and tea. Who needs that? For our family of seven, that's $14—just to drink Pepsi! If your family must drink soda or tea, drink it at home. You can purchase it much cheaper on sale at the grocery store. But for eating out, stick with water. It's free and it's healthy.

∽

Question:

I love the idea of getting online coupons, but I hate the idea of getting all the junk e-mail that I know will start coming. What can I do to still get the savings but not bog down my e-mail inbox?

Answer:

That's an easy one! It's a good idea to set up a junk e-mail address to use when you sign up for offers online. This keeps your work and personal e-mails free of the junk e-mail that invariably arrives once you sign up at a site. They'll sell your address to one site, and they'll sell it to another, and so on and so on and so on. Give your junk e-mail address when you sign up for offers and save your primary e-mail account for your friends. Usually, you can set up an extra account with your regular Internet provider, or sign up for a free e-mail account with Gmail or Yahoo! mail.

Question:

How do you keep track of all your coupons and savings items? It sounds like you have to be extremely organized. And I'm not! Any quick tips?

Answer:

I have a coupon box that is a plastic shoe-sized container with a snap-on lid. There are basically two ways to organize your coupons—categorically or alphabetically. I prefer alphabetical tabs, and I file the coupon by the name that is most prominent on the coupon. For example, "All" laundry soap is filed under A. If you have the alphabetical approach instead of the categorical approach, then you don't have to remember if you filed your Horizon organic milk coupons under the Dairy category or the Beverage area. You also don't have to wade through the Soap category and sort through laundry soap, bar soap, and liquid hand soap to finally find the Electrosol automatic dishwasher soap.

You can just go straight to the E section of your alphabetical tabs.

At the end of each month, pull out your expired coupons and send them to military families stationed overseas (who can use these up to six months past the expiration date). Just e-mail assistant@elliekay.com to get a list of military bases that could use your donations.

For restaurant coupons, I have a fabric coupon holder that is about the size of my wallet and carry it with me in my purse. That way, I don't have to cart a shoe-sized coupon box into Mimi's Café to have lunch with my girlfriend!

Question:

I don't know, Ellie. All these coupons and ad circulars just to go to the grocery store seems like a lot of work! I do okay taking advantage of the in-store savings. Why go to all the trouble to save on 10 and 15 cents-off coupons?

Answer:

I can see you still need some convincing—even though you've seen how much I've saved my family by using the above methods. You can Google "Cost of Food at Home" to find a complete chart on the most updated food costs. Trust me, the time you'll expend on saving and clipping coupons will amaze you. I make the equivalent of $150 per hour by clipping coupons!

5

Save Big on Clothing
and Dry Cleaning

12-Minute Tip #4: Make the most of clearance sales. When shopping the clearance rack at your favorite store at the mall, be sure to take twelve minutes to ask the salesperson to check the stockroom or check with other stores for the size you need. Waiting while they check stock routinely saves us $40 per pair of jeans that are on sale for $20 for our teens. Multiply this by four pairs of jeans per year for our seven family members and you have a savings of $1,120.

My motto is *"I may dress our family from consignment stores—but we don't have to look like it!"* And we don't. As a matter of fact, several years ago I was dressing my then seven-year-old daughter Bethany for church. As I was pinning on her tiger pin (that I got for 10 cents), she told me, "Mama, the week before the ice storm something happened in Sunday school."

She adjusted the bow on her head (25 cents) and pulled her new black tights out of the package (15 cents). "My friend Caitlyn asked me a question."

I straightened the collar on her black velvet dress ($3). "What did she ask?"

"Why I always wear such beautiful clothes."

I helped put on her full-length, black-and-white plaid, fully lined wool coat ($6). "What did you tell her?"

She looked at me in the mirror and flashed a dimpled smile. "Why, I said 'thank you,' of course!"

Her secret was safe with me.

There's nothing wrong with shopping at name-brand stores, and there's certainly nothing wrong with quality. My closet is full of name-brand clothing paid for by a dime on the dollar—or less. Still my wardrobe consists of quality clothing to be worn to special functions, church, receptions, dinners, dances, formals, seminars, and even the local gym!

In fact you can save 30 to 90 percent on clothing without sacrificing quality or style by shopping consignment stores and even garage sales.

If you're like most Americans, you'll spend $1,760 per year on clothing, which breaks down to about $147 a month (about 5 percent of your monthly spending). If you're single with no children or dependents, $147 doesn't seem too bad. But what if you have multiple people to shop for or dry clean for?

The most obvious way to save money on clothing is to buy it used. Some people are squeamish about germs or thinking used clothing is dirty. If you are one of these, wash it in hot (120 degrees) water, and you'll get rid of any germs or dirt. Do you ever try on clothing at a department store, even though someone probably tried it on before you?

Even so, never fear, there is room for new clothes in a

bargain hunter's closet, and I have quite a few. But we'll look at buying new after we've finished looking at buying used.

∽

Consignment Stores/Garage Sales/ Thrift Shops

⌘ I know this may seem like a callous first tip, especially coming from a loving mother of many, but if you're going garage-saling—forget the kids! You'll leave at 0'dark hundred and you need to concentrate. Admittedly, there will be times when you'll have to take along the munchkins. But if at all possible, it's best to leave them with a friend or at home with your spouse. You want to get an early start before the best bargains are gone.

⌘ If it's damaged, leave it. You can afford to be choosy. If it's dirty, you can wash it. If it's stained and you can't tell whether it's permanent or not—then leave it on the table. Last week you were paying full price at a department store! This week you don't have to settle for a pair of jeans with an oil stain on them. Look for clothing with the original sales tags still on them and products in their original packaging. Or pay attention to the nearly new clothing. My friend Ginger purchased five name-brand, barely worn work suits from a garage sale for $10 each. The woman who sold them had purchased them just before she found out she was pregnant. Since she

decided to quit her job to stay home with her baby,
she obviously didn't need the suits anymore. Ginger
got a great deal, appears professional, and looks like
she spent almost a hundred dollars on each outfit.

▨ Check the zippers, buttons, and snaps on clothing.
Check the knees on jeans to determine wear and
tear.

▨ In a consignment store, get to know the owner. Then
he or she can help you find the kind of clothing you
need most. Some shops even keep a card file that
lists your size as well as the style and color of clothing you are looking for.

New Clothes

▨ Before heading out to the store, do the latest cool
thing and "shop your closet" by looking through
your clothes and taking inventory of your present
wardrobe. Some of the clothes that you haven't been
getting enough use of may simply need to be altered,
repaired, or dry-cleaned—thereby saving you a lot of
money over buying something new. When you shop
your closet, make note of the items you need most
and their sizes.

▨ Buy classic, long-lasting styles rather than fads.

▨ Check out the care label. Instead of buying clothing
that has to be dry-cleaned, pressed, and starched—
try buying easy-care clothing. Sometimes you don't
have a choice, but often you can just as easily choose
a wash-and-wear article of clothing as a dry-clean-
only item. The time you spend running to the dry

Did You Know?

If garage sales aren't your thing, thrift shops are an excellent alternative. Thrift shops may charge higher prices than garage sales, but they have a greater selection. There's also the full gamut of thrift stores—from those that you never want to visit to the ones I saw in Palm Springs where you feel you need to let them run a credit check before you qualify to enter the store! Also, most thrift shops have a place to try on clothing, so you can better determine fit and style. Some thrift shops have specials—half-price days or buy-one-get-one-free days, among others. Thrift shops are also great places to get "in between" clothes. My friend Ginger was losing weight and didn't want to spend $35 for new jeans every time she went down a pants size, so she purchased name-brand jeans on the special half-price days. She was able to get four pairs for what it would cost for one in a department store! And a few pair still had the tags on them—they were new and had never been worn. That's a great deal!

Consignment shops have the greatest selection but the most expensive prices for used clothing. They are often twice as high as a thrift shop (making them four times as high as a garage sale). However, their prices on formal attire and business clothing are hard to beat.

cleaners and the $10 to $15 you save on your weekly laundry bill is well worth the choice.

- ✄ *Never* buy clothes on credit. *Just don't do it!* You only dig a deeper hole and create more financial stress.

- ⧉ If you buy clothing before the season begins or in season, you'll probably *pay* top dollar. If you buy your clothes at midseason or end-of-the-season clearance sales, you'll *save* top dollar.
- ⧉ Try to buy quality clothing: check the seams, zippers, buttons, and fabric weight before you buy.
- ⧉ Stock up on accessories on December 26. Often you can get great deals on accessories, such as jewelry, right after Christmas. I know a woman who shops at her local discount department store the two or three days after Christmas and buys the gift sets of jewelry and lotions for herself. Save up to 75 percent off the original prices.
- ⧉ In men's suits, stick with conservative styles and dark colors. Select wool or wool blends to extend the life of the suit and increase the wearing opportunities. Also, see the following tip for suits in the "Dry Cleaning" section.

Dry Cleaning

- ⧉ This seems to go without saying, but I'll say it anyway. Take care of the clothes you have and pay special attention to the care instructions on the label. Use Woolite for sweaters and lay them out to dry.
- ⧉ To save 75 percent on dry cleaning, use a coin-operated dry-cleaning machine or a dry-cleaning product you can use in your dryer instead of commercial cleaners.
- ⧉ Always hang up suits in an open space after wear, and air them out for twenty-four hours before put-

---

Did You Know?

Not all outlet stores are equal. There is a trend in America for the discount outlet mall; you'll find one in every large city and throughout suburbia. Watch these outlets carefully. Just because they are billed as bargain outlets does not mean they are bargain stores. I don't consider paying $75 for a $95 casual shirt saving money. The way I see it, that's spending money. When you happen upon a real outlet, though, you've got it made! These outlets offer values that range from 40 percent to 95 percent off retail prices. As always, look carefully for damaged zippers, etc., and consider each piece and its price. I've found some truly awesome outlet stores that rival the prices found at garage sales.

In Tuscaloosa, Alabama, I gave a seminar and had time to visit the Goody's Clearance Outlet. Most of the things were 75 percent off the lowest ticketed price. It took me three hours to get through the whole store. But when I was finished, I'd bought sixty articles of new clothing—or $350 dollars worth—for $52. Now that's what I call saving money!

---

ting them back in the closet—it helps minimize dry-cleaning costs.

❈ Before you store your clothes for the season, make sure they are clean. This prevents permanent stains and ensures their usefulness and readiness for the next season.

Baby Items

▤ You'll go through a ton of baby wipes in the course
of a month. If you can't find them on sale or if
they're still too expensive with a coupon, a Web
buck, or a store coupon, then consider making your
own. Check out my special recipe on page 16 in
chapter 2 under "Baby Room."

▤ Buy disposable diapers. Yes, you read that right! If
you are considering going with cloth diapers to save
money, then think this through again because you
won't save money after laundering and the initial investment of cloth diapers. However, if you choose
cloth for sustainable purposes, then you go, girl!

▤ Only buy diapers that are on sale and with a coupon.
Also check out www.valuepage.com for Web bucks,
which can give you cash back on the diapers you purchase, good on your next shopping trip. You could
get Web bucks for diapers you would buy anyway;
every dollar adds up on this costly expense for babies.

▤ To get your favorite manufacturer's coupons, sign up
at your doctor's office for diaper promotions from
the leading brands. They should start sending you
coupons, usually with an informative booklet or
magazine, every one or two months.

▤ Go to your favorite brand's Web site by typing
www.(brandname).com. For example, www.pampers
.com or www.huggies.com or www.luvs.com. Many
of these sites will even have gift certificates available
for purchase, which is a practical, money-saving gift
to request. Or call the toll-free number on the diaper
packaging and ask them to send coupons to you.

CHILDREN'S CLOTHING

⊞ Buy used clothing. Get over the idea that Junior has
  to be dressed in brand-new clothing that he'll grow
  out of in a month! You can buy used clothing and
  not deprive your child. Check out garage sales,
  which can be your best bargains.

⊞ Barter. Don't be afraid to ask your sister or a friend
  for her baby clothes, especially if you know they just
  had their last child. If it makes you (and them) feel
  better, then offer to barter for the trade.

⊞ Trade off some of your children's clothing with
  a family who has kids in corresponding sizes.
  For example, the Brazell family has a seven-
  year-old boy and a nine-year-old girl. They
  trade their outgrown clothing with the Taylor
  family, who has a six-year-old boy and a ten-year-
  old girl.

Did You Know?

*Babies' and younger children's clothing is worn, on the
average, for only six weeks! Do you think a baby could
wear out his clothes in that amount of time?*

*One mom asked me, "Ooh, I don't know how I
feel about used clothing for my child." I said, "Tell me,
do you take brand-new sheets with you when you go
stay at the Marriott? Don't you sleep on used sheets
there?"*

*What's the difference? The difference is about a 50
to 85 percent savings.*

❧

Question:
I've found some great deals online. How safe is it to purchase online?

Answer:
You're right about finding great deals online. I've purchased lots of items online and have not had a problem with any safety or identity theft issues because I make sure the site is secure. It's best to be smart about where you're purchasing and how reputable that business is. Here are a few things to keep in mind so you don't get taken. (For a more in-depth discussion of ways to protect you and your family from identity theft, pick up a copy of my book *Living Rich for Less*.)

- Check the Internet Fraud Information Center (www.fraud.org) or the Better Business Bureau (www.bbb.org) for any information about the Web site you're considering purchasing from.
- You should be able to contact the retailer through a variety of methods, including e-mail, telephone, and live interactive chat.
- The retailer should prominently display customer service options throughout the Web site so you have no difficulty finding them.
- You should expect responsive and prompt replies from your retailer regardless of how you contact them.
- The customer service agent should be knowledgeable and equipped to answer your questions.

- Steer clear of new companies. If a company is new, chances are it is still working out the kinks at your expense.
- Look carefully at legal disclaimers. Some say they have the right to take up to three weeks to notify you if they're out of stock, which could make you three weeks late on your project.
- Beware of early billing. Some stores invoice you before you receive the merchandise. Make sure your credit card is charged at the same time the product is shipped and not before. And if you get a second invoice before you get the item, cancel the order.
- Pay with a credit card instead of debit card or check. Using a credit card provides more legal protection if a dispute arises.
- Read the warranty before buying an item, and check for limits on the company's liability if something goes wrong with the item.
- Make a printout of the Web page, the item being purchased, the warranty, and any messages between you and the seller.
- Only give away name, address, and credit card information to a secure site or a site that will not allow third parties to view the information in transit. All secured sites are indicated by an *s* after the http address in the browser box, or a closed lock or unbroken key appears as a symbol of a secure site.

6

Save Big on Recreation and Entertainment

12-Minute Tip #5: Go take a hike! Hiking is a great way to combine exercise with family and friend connection time. Discover the countryside around you. You'll be amazed at what's on your doorstep. Take twelve minutes to search "Hiking Trails" on the Internet for a multitude of ideas. For a complete "what, when, where, and how" of hiking and walking, go to http://dir.yahoo.com/recreation/outdoors/hiking, or for a full listing of national parks, go to www.nps.gov/parks.html. For state searches of hundreds of leisure activities on federal lands, go to www.recreation.gov. By hiking monthly instead of paying the price for season tickets to your local theme park, plus the cost of parking and food at those pricey places, you can save $1,200 per year.

I can always tell when Bob is reading the Sunday comics. His guffaws echo throughout the house. Indeed, he laughs so loud, the neighbors hear him. It gives them something *else* to talk about. He has fun reading the comics, and the kids enjoy watching him. They make microwave popcorn and pull up chairs. The truth be told, this is the real reason we're late to church on Sunday mornings.

When Bob is confronted with his embarrassing guffawing habit, his explanation is straightforward. "It takes so little to keep an idiot happy." Life's simple pleasures *truly* are the best.

Of course we were all happy for those moments when everyone in our family was entertained by Bob. But what about the other days and hours? We couldn't just always sit around watching Papa read and guffaw. So we got creative. We wanted to have fun but definitely not break the bank.

If you're like the average American, according to a recent Gallup poll, you spend $176 a month on recreation and entertainment—and that's not counting eating out.[1] Considering you should be spending only 2 percent of your monthly income on recreation and entertainment, um, this could become a problem. Quickly.

Add to that amount the cost of eating out, and the evening of delight can end up being short-lived when you don't have money to pay for things like gas or mortgage. Although I covered most cost-cutting measures for eating out in chapter 4, I do include some food-related activities here in case you're anything like our family. When we go out for recreation or entertainment, we often include some sort of eating. Here are some ways to keep grownups and kids alike happily entertained—on a shoestring, of course.

⤴

Inside Activities

▦ Every once in a while just skip the movie theater or
the video store. Check out Netflix. This online
DVD and Blu-ray disk rental service offers a flat-rate
rental-by-mail and online streaming. It has a collection of a hundred thousand titles, so you can find
hundreds of family-friendly options. Beware that
this is a membership-based business. But you can go
with the limited plan at $4.99 a month that offers
one DVD at a time, with a limit of two per month,
plus the ability to watch up to two hours of movies
(some new releases) and TV episodes (including the
current season) online.

▦ Better yet, save even more money by checking
out the library. Sure, everyone thinks of it as being
a place for great books. But it's so much more
than that. The library is a great source of entertainment. You can borrow videos, DVDs, audio books,
and CDs, plus the ever-popular books. Many
libraries offer free classes, author readings, book
clubs, and guest lectures. Some even have movie
nights or afternoons. Try researching your family
tree at a library with a good genealogy reference
section. Save up to $50 by hitting the library for
your movie-watching needs and skipping the
theater.

▦ Ditch the cable company and plug in your computer
to your TV set. Watch your television shows online.
Save $100. I know one family of four who cancelled
their cable service, going with just the basic channels.
They now watch their favorite shows online (check

out the TV channels' Web sites or a site like www.hulu
.com, which offers current and older shows for free).
And the best part (besides obviously saving money)
is that you have more of a choice over what your
children get to watch, how often, and for how long.

- ▣ Consolidate your magazine subscriptions. Magazines
  that are taking up space could possibly be consolidated or even canceled. Consider sharing a subscrip-
  tion with a friend or relative; the average American
  subscribes to two to three magazines that they never
  read. This can save $90 per year.

- ▣ Rediscover the lost art of game playing. You know all
  those games you got as kids for Christmas and birthday presents? They're just taking up space on a shelf
  when they could be a great source of entertainment
  and together time for you and your family or
  friends. My youngest, Joshua, and I just played
  Scrabble last night. It not only gives us some quality
  bonding time, but it's improving his vocabulary as
  well. Because he's the "baby," he hasn't wised up to
  what the other family members have learned: never
  play Scrabble with a professional writer!

- ▣ Speaking of playing games... How about making up
  your own games based on some of the game shows
  on TV? Create your own versions of *Jeopardy* or
  Family Feud and see how much you can learn about
  your family and friends.

OUT ON THE TOWN

- ▣ Like to golf but can't because the greens fee is too
  expensive? Go to the driving range.

Did You Know? —————————————

According to a recent Gallup poll, most Americans would spend their discretionary income on "grownup" toys— mainly in the form of recreation and entertainment.[2]

⊞ While many concerts are quite pricey, some are free or available at discounts. Check your local paper for tickets that are being sold or the lineup for a free concert series. Check out the local college and high schools. They do great concerts for great prices.

⊞ I talked about the Entertainment or Happenings book in chapter 4. But don't forget that you can use it for recreation as well! Save $17,000 on dining out, movie tickets, theme park entrance fees, and local shopping.

⊞ Subscribe to www.travelzoo.com's "Top 20" and you'll not only get the lowdown on the best vacation values of the week, but the ending section always has discounted offers on traveling Broadway shows, local theaters, and special events at discounted prices.

⊞ Get a zoo or museum membership. It usually pays for itself after two or three visits. For more information on using your membership on vacation in other locales, see chapter 7.

⊞ Cheer on your local Little League teams. You're getting involved in the community and it's free. That's a home run!

⊞ Have a celebrity photo shoot afternoon. With digital cameras, you can take hundreds of photos at a time. Go somewhere fun—the mall, a park, your town's downtown center—and shoot away. Then download the photos on your computer and connect it to your television for a slideshow.

- Combine activities. Killing two birds with one stone is one of my favorite pastimes. I like to take a walk and visit with a friend at the same time. It accomplishes two important functions—exercise of the legs and the jaws.
- Consider investing in a family pool pass at your local park district. Swimming is one of our favorite sports. Of course when our boys Joshua and Jonathan were young, we were never sure when they were going to entertain the entire crowd by removing their swimsuits in the middle of the pool area.

Did You Know?

Volunteering as a dog-walker at your local animal shelter or humane society is a meaningful way to make a difference in the lives of homeless dogs in your community. It will also bring you great joy, and it's absolutely, 100 percent free.

Dogs in animal shelters are confined to cages.[3] *So by volunteering to be a dog-walker, you get exercise and you provide exercise, affection, and socialization that confined dogs need to stay healthy, happy, and adoptable.*

Most shelters allow volunteer dog-walkers, who have completed an orientation, simply to drop by during regular business hours to walk and play with the dogs. Go to www.pets911.com/organizations or www.petfinder.com and enter your zip code to find your local animal shelter.

FOOD-RELATED ACTIVITIES

⚏ Have a themed evening. If you decide to do Asian food, serve it on a low coffee table and don't wear your shoes. See if you can find robes that would be similar to a kimono and don't forget the chopsticks! Or serve Italian on a red-and-white-checked cloth with a candle in a bottle and Italian music playing in the background. If you want the feeling of the great outdoors, serve a fried chicken dinner on a table-cloth placed on the floor with fresh flowers in vases around you.

Did You Know?

Did you know that the average mom spends only 12.9 hours per week with her child (and that's not all one-on-one time), and the average dad spends only 6.5 hours per week? And the average working parent spends only 19 minutes per day with her children.[4] I believe that the main reason for this is because many families don't eat meals together since everyone is so busy. So prioritize eating together, and when you do, make a point of interacting with each child. At our dinner table we ask each one about his or her day, and then at the end of the meal, our tradition is to have everyone share their favorite part of the day. The kids used to try to share their least favorite part of the day, but we didn't allow it because we wanted to keep things positive.

- Buy a half-gallon of your favorite ice cream. Take it to a park, throw down a blanket, and eat the entire thing! It's cheaper than multiple single scoops from Baskin-Robbins!

- Who says we have to go to a full-service restaurant and first-run movie in order to have fun? You can cook a nice meal at home, and you don't have to spend $50 to $100 on it. If you want to invite several couples or families, make it a potluck. Pick a theme—like a Mexican Fiesta or Country Western potluck.

- If you just want to get away for a while, pick the bargain matinee or dollar theater and eat dessert afterward.

- Better yet, go out for ice cream and rent a DVD for the night. First-run movies will often make it to the video market while they are still playing in the dollar theater and in as little as nine months. We go to www.pluggedinonline.com to monitor their recommendations for younger viewers. It's easier to turn off a $4 DVD than it is to walk out on a $50 family night movie at the theater.

- If you go to the theater, pass on the sodas and popcorn—I've heard some of that stuff is life threatening anyway. Save as much as $30.

- If you want to take the family out for dinner, check the local restaurants for specials. Family nights are sometimes offered on Tuesdays or Wednesdays. For example, when we lived in New Mexico, a restaurant in our area had a Tuesday night special where kids ate for free. There was a limit of two free kids' meals per one adult meal. Since our two youngest never finished their food, we would split a dinner between them. We fed the whole family a great meal at a full-service restaurant—with ice cream—for around $12, which included a 20 percent tip based on the price before coupons and specials.

❧

Question:

My husband loves basketball. I was thinking about surprising him by purchasing season tickets to our city's professional basketball team. But the season tickets are ridiculously expensive. Is there anything I can do to save money but still have a good surprise for him?

Answer:

I usually try to find a smarter way to buy just about anything, and season tickets are no exception. One thing you can do is to go in with another family on these tickets. Most come in pairs, and you can split the cost with a friend whose husband has a passion for B-ball too! Divide the tickets at the beginning of the season by taking turns picking the games they will attend. On one occasion, both guys can go together; on other occasions (an anniversary, for example) one of the couples can go; and in still other instances a father and son or daughter might attend. Each guy picks the dates that are most important to him as they take turns.

Another idea is to go to a local financial social media site such as www.fatwallet.com or www.craigslist.org.

These sites may offer discounted season tickets from other individuals. A word of caution about Craigslist—it's not well monitored and there are some seedy elements to that site, so be careful and don't send kids there! Also check with local charities that have an annual auction and see if they are auctioning off season tickets. You might pick up a bargain and help a charity at the same time. A final idea is to opt for a minor league team in a different sport. We have Triple-A baseball in our area and those tickets are very affordable—after all, it's the thought that counts, right?

Question:

Our kids go to a nice Christian school that we have budgeted and even sacrificed for them to be able to attend. Some of the kids there come from very wealthy families and spend their recreation time going to expensive plays, pricey restaurants, and professional sporting events where they drop an easy $500 or more to take their family for a night out. How can we compete with the Joneses without feeling like the poor kids on the block?

Answer:

We've been in this same position at times with our kids too! One of the things we do is to stress the idea that our family is unique. We don't use the word *special* because it seems to have a negative connotation with our teens, so we just say our family is a "one of a kind." We stress all the cool things that make our family different, such as the fact that our kids have parents who are really involved in their lives and spend time with them. One example is that we go camping and can all quote lines from our favorite movies.

These are things our kids value, and by putting the emphasis on how we are "one of a kind," we are able to contrast what we do with what the Joneses do: "We may not go to The Ritz for dinner, but our s'mores around the campfire are unbeatable!"

7

Save Big on Vacations

12-Minute Tip #6: Subscribe to a site, such as www.travelzoo.com, that will alert you to travel and entertainment values as soon as they go on sale. There are often limited quantities available, so be prepared to act quickly. We were alerted to a four-day Mexican-Caribbean cruise on sale from $1,450 per person to only *$199*. This took a few minutes to book and saved us $2,500 off the regular price. So take twelve minutes a week to review these top twenty tips and save $1,200 on vacations this year!

I get more mileage out of a quarter than a Hyundai gets out of a gas can. You see, I'm a born saver. I started saving money so early in life that by the time I was twelve years old, I'd saved enough to fund a trip to Spain to visit my cousins. I took three rolls of film with me and only snapped six pictures, thereby "saving" two and one-half rolls! Okay, I guess I used to be a little compulsive about saving.

On the other hand, my husband, Bob, is a born spender. When he was a kid, his paper route money never saw the inside of his pocket. This pattern continued into his adult years, and when he became a fighter pilot in the Air Force, he could still spend money faster than his Stealth

F-117 could go from 0 to 500 miles per hour. For you Air Force novices, that's pretty fast!

The thing both of us discovered was that you don't have to become a miser or spend a lot of money to make your vacation special, even if your schedules or finances prohibit you from taking a trip.

Too many people fall into either going hog wild and putting the vacation of their dreams on a credit card because "the memories we'll make are more important" or they put the kibosh on doing anything for a vacation because "we can't afford it." Be assured, there is a happy medium!

When you're planning a vacation, you should make sure that you set aside 2 percent of your monthly income. That may not seem like a lot of money, but you'd be surprised what kind of vacation you can take on that low of an amount. Be creative and you'll have fun—*without* going into debt! Here's how.

&

- Decide exactly how much you're going to spend before you pull out of the driveway. Determine what activities take priority and make a pact, as a family, to *stay within those spending limits.*
- Travel off-season. By traveling during an off-peak time you'll not only save money, you won't fight the crowds either. According to Consumer Reports Travel Letter, the optimum time to get the best airline fares is October through early December and January through March. The fares are even better if you stay over a Saturday night. Bob and I went to Ireland in January, which was considered the off-

season. Everything was *still* green! We enjoyed a full-value vacation for half price by going in January instead of July.

Did You Know?

One reason people overspend on vacations is because they fail to plan ahead. They arrive at their destination and take in unplanned tourist attractions, eat at specialty restaurants, and buy overpriced souvenirs that inevitably end up collecting dust or taking up space in the back of closets and drawers. This failure to plan ahead costs hundreds, if not thousands, of extra dollars each year.

AIRFARE

- Don't pay full price on airfare. Check online for great deals. Go to www.bookingbuddy.com, a site that will check all the standard search engine sites. This site will save you time since it will search such major sites as Travelocity, Expedia, Priceline, Orbitz, and CheapTickets. When you find the best price, you can book directly on that site with a link from www.bookingbuddy.com. Save an average of $100 per ticket per person.
- Other Internet sites you can check include: www.bestfares.com and www.smarterliving.com. Once you find the best fares at these Web sites, go to the original airline's site to check for even better deals.

⚏ Try the airlines directly for their Internet specials.
   Most major U.S. carriers offer weekly or last-minute
   specials. You can try American Airlines' Net SAAvers
   at www.aa.com, US Airways' e-Savers at www.us
   airways.com, United's E-Fares at www.ual.com, or
   Northwest Airlines' CyberSavers at www.nwa.com. I
   also tried Southwest Airlines at www.southwest.com
   for their Click 'n Save Specials. I booked two round-
   trip, nonstop tickets from El Paso to Dallas for a
   total of $220 (only $110 each). The catch is that I
   had to buy well in advance, and the tickets were
   nonrefundable and nonchangeable. However, on
   Southwest I could still cancel the tickets and use that
   money toward another flight as long as I did so
   within a twelve-month period.

⚏ Timing is everything when you purchase your tickets. The best day of the week to buy is usually
   Wednesday. At 1:00 a.m. So set your alarm! The
   worst day? Late in the day on Friday. So unless
   you're notified of a major sale by a travel site, try to
   avoid booking your tickets over a weekend.

⚏ Think about the balance of a good airfare with a
   good hotel rate. For example, even though airfare to
   Chicago can be cheap (they have two major airports
   that are served by dozens of airlines), city hotel costs
   can be steep. Finding a cheaper hotel at an auction
   site, such as eBay or Priceline, and the airfare at a
   travel site could be the best value. You can also combine airfare and hotel at some of these sites and save
   more.

⚏ Look for last-minute deals. If your schedule is flexible, take advantage of the last-minute deals offered

by airlines and hotels. Moment's Notice is a booking specialist (www.moments-notice.com or 1-888-241-3366) that charges an annual fee of $25 but boasts bargain-basement prices and some of the best values for cruises: Europe, Rio de Janeiro, and certain parts of the Caribbean. If you buy a red-eye special for substantial savings, sometimes you can show up at the ticket counter early and see if they can schedule you on an earlier flight. At times, I've been able to get a really inexpensive upgrade to first class for as little as $35 when I take a red-eye.

Did You Know?

Many airlines now board everyone according to a certain group number. So if you're listed in group 6, you're one of the last, after groups 1 through 5. In order to rank in an earlier group, take advantage of checking in as soon as you can—which is usually twenty-four hours before the flight—or select seats that are part of an earlier boarding group. Those who board last may have to check their carry-ons, which is a hassle. You can check in on the airline's Web site for seating charts and policies.

HOTEL

▦ You can often find packages for great hotel rates at the airline Internet site when you book travel. I've found that I can get an even better rate at the www.southwest.com site on hotels than I would get if I bid on a room at other travel sites. So when you're checking airline fares, be sure to check hotel (and car rental rates!) as well. You can also look on hotel sites for their weekly Internet specials. Try the following for e-mail alerts: Hyatt at www.hyatt.com, Radisson at www.radisson.com, Holiday Inn at www.holidayinn.com, Best Western at www .bestwestern.com, and Hilton at www.hilton.com.

▣ For last-minute hotel rooms, you could go to the very large TravelWeb site at www.travelweb.com. While you're there, click on Pricebreakers for new travel deals added daily.

Creative Trips

▣ If you have friends you like *a lot* and you think your friendship can survive the test of a family vacation, then double up with that family and cut your bills in half. The Grimes and the Mortons tried it and saved a bundle—and loved the experience so much they made it an every-other-year tradition. The normal price of a weeklong mountain cabin rental with three bedrooms was $1,900.

You don't have to rent a cabin to double up with another family. You can find many different kinds of rentals at www.findrental.com. Suite hotels that offer extra rooms are also an option, such as the ones found at www.orbitz.com or www.cheaprooms.com.

If you love the great outdoors, consider sharing campsite fees or RV rentals to split the price of a

---

Did You Know?

If you travel a lot for business and/or pleasure, it's important to stay at the same brand of hotels in order to maximize your "frequent stayer" status. Be sure to check out the brand's Web site for the requirements as well as the benefits for each level. For example, I try to stay at the Hilton family of hotels and didn't realize that I could have achieved "Diamond" status last year instead of just my "Gold" status by dividing my stays a bit more strategically. It was all in the way we booked the hotels.

In addition, you may qualify for benefits that you won't get unless you ask for them when you check into the hotel. I routinely ask for upgrades to a suite, and they are often available. But when I fail to ask, they usually don't volunteer to upgrade me. It's the old adage, "You have not because you ask not." This holds true for free breakfasts, bottles of water, and discount spa services that may be yours for the asking.

---

camping adventure. If you're camping a week or more, you can save $1,250 in rental fees and $2,500 in general expenses (even more if you share the cooking chores and eat in).

- ⌘ Rent an RV and cook in versus staying at a hotel and eating out. At www.rvrental.com you can find rentals across the country that range from $117 to $385 per day. Depending on the RV's owner, other charges to consider are hospitality kits, kitchen kits, and emergency road kits. Cleaning fees will apply if the RV is not returned in the condition in which it was rented. Save an average of $500 per week.

⌖ Consider volunteering. Mac and Dina Thompson went to a private campground in Colorado and fell in love with the staff, landscape, and activities. They also caught the vision of how combining volunteering with a vacation could help teach their kids the concept of servant missions. And instead of paying $1,000 for the week, they had a working vacation for free.

Not all campgrounds offer this kind of trade-off, but if your family enjoys this environment, it would be worth your time to contact a local retreat center or campground. Or go to www.acacamps.org for the American Camp Association to find a location near you.

Wilderness Volunteers (www.wilderness volunteers.org) offers people a chance to help maintain national parks, forests, and wilderness areas across the United States. You can do everything from trail maintenance to re-vegetation projects. You will need to provide your own camping gear and share campsite chores. Most Wilderness Volunteer trips last about a week and cost around $219.

⌖ Take a learning vacation. At Shaw Guides (www .shawguides.com), they'll match you with a learning vacation around the world, while Elderhostel (www.elderhostel.org) offers those fifty-five and older up to ten thousand options, starting at as little as $556 for a six-day photography workshop in Massachusetts.

⛿ Select vacation areas in your locale. Try to see everything in your area.

Did You Know?

If you have kids, allowing everybody in the family to have a say in vacation options can, believe it or not, make paying cash for the entire trip easier—and can save you 20 percent, or $750 from the average $2,500 vacation. Each person on the trip gets a set amount of cash to use however he or she wants—souvenirs, excursions, special events, and even food. Not only does it keep your spending in check, but it is a fun and practical way to teach your children about finances. (In Living Rich for Less, *I spend an entire section on the importance of getting the family on board with vacations and practical tips on how to have fun as a family both in planning for the trip and taking it).*

DAY TRIPS

⛿ Plan day trips to area sites and save the cost of a hotel room. Get out your map and look at day trips you can take. You may be surprised at how many fascinating little towns are within a short distance from your home. You can enjoy going to look at historic buildings, architecture, gardens, or wander around markets and antique stores.

⛿ Pack your lunch on day trips and have a great time relaxing at a roadside picnic table.

▣ Remember those zoo and museum memberships we mentioned in chapter 6? They're great money savers on vacation too. Most zoos and museums are members of reciprocal associations. This means you pay a fee with the zoo or museum of your choice and you get reciprocal privileges in several hundred other zoos, aquariums, wildlife parks, and museums.

When we lived in Alamogordo, New Mexico, we bought a family membership to our local zoo for $25 per year. With that membership card we also went to the El Paso Zoo (it would have cost $18 for the family for the day), the Albuquerque Biological Park (saved $23 for the day), and the Los Angeles Zoo (saved $34). As a matter of fact, we maintained our zoo membership when we moved from New Mexico to New York and got free entrance to zoos in New York for less than the annual membership of our local zoo.

Check out the Association of Zoos and Aquariums at www.aza.org, where you can view the several hundred zoos available in this reciprocal zoo program. And you can search just about every museum in the country by area if you go to www.museumca.org.

FOREIGN TRAVEL

▣ Forgo traveler's checks, which cost an average of $1 per $100 (most travelers buy $1,500 worth). Save $15 on fees and an average of 10 cents on the dollar for credit card exchange rates (versus cash) and savings on fee services for exchange. This is a savings of

---

Did You Know? ─────────────────────────

With an economic downturn, vacationing from home becomes the least expensive and often most fun option. Many people take all the great local opportunities for granted, never visiting them because, well, because there will always be "someday." Enjoy the trips and then in the evenings, you can journal about them or scrapbook them to remind you how much fun your area can be.

$300 on $3,000 worth of hotel fees, rentals, gifts, tickets, etc. The two save a total of $315.

🔢 Take a credit card with a 1 percent fee rather than 3 percent for $3,000 worth of overseas transactions. That will reduce currency-conversion fees. These fees are as obnoxious as an $8 cup of coffee, but they can drive up the cost of your trip overseas if you're not careful. For example, Visa and MasterCard charge a standard 1 percent fee for foreign purchases. In recent years, many banks have tacked on currency-conversion fees of up to 2 percent. These fees are calculated as a percentage of your overall credit card purchase, usually in U.S. dollars. For example, if you spent 100 British pounds and it converted to $198 in U.S. dollars, a 3 percent currency-conversion fee would add about $6. These additional fees are avoidable. Call your credit card companies and find out what their transaction fees are and ask if they'll charge a lower fee. Then use your card with the lowest fees. Save $60.

⚅ Avoid cash in foreign countries. As annoying as conversion fees may be on your credit card purchases, using cash can cost you even more. Credit card companies can negotiate a better exchange rate than you can get on your own. In the overall scheme of things, 3 percent on a credit card is still less than you'll pay if you take traveler's checks, and it's a lot less than you'd pay if you exchange currency at a U.S. airport.

⚅ Use ATMs to acquire foreign currency for tips, taxis, and other items you cannot charge on credit cards. You will get a better exchange rate than you can at a foreign currency exchange.

⚅ Before you go overseas, research your bank's Web site to find out which brands of ATMs are in its network for the country you are visiting. This will save on ATM withdrawal fees.

⚅ When getting cash with your debit or ATM cards, look for European banks rather than commercial exchange counters—you'll get a better rate.

⚅ Do not use your credit card to get cash from an ATM. Nearly 90 percent of credit cards charge a higher interest rate for cash advances than for credit card purchases, with some charging more than 28 percent, according to Consumer Action's annual credit card survey.

⚅ Minimize the number of cash exchanges you make as there are usually processing, servicing, and administrative fees assessed on each transaction. Some exchanges or banks may even offer a better exchange rate on larger amounts of money.

⌘ Remember that there is no grace period with credit
   card cash advances. Interest starts accruing from the
   day you get your money. This is in addition to the
   fee your credit card company may charge for the
   cash advance.
⌘ Reject offers from merchants to convert your bill
   into dollars. You'll still have to pay the currency-
   conversion fee charged by your credit card, and
   the merchant may add his own conversion fee
   of 2 percent to 3 percent!

Did You Know?

*America has some of the most traveler-friendly policies
in the world. So don't assume other countries are the
same. Before you travel to a foreign destination, be sure
to check with your travel agent or airline provider for
baggage rules in other countries. We went to Europe
only to discover that their carry-on policy was very limited, which meant we had to check more bags and the
extra baggage fees were as high as some of the airfares!
So the key to managing your baggage in foreign countries is to travel as light as possible or be prepared to pay
the high price!*

CRUISING

⌘ Subscribe to the "Weekly Top 20" on www.travel
   zoo.com, and be prepared to act fast once you get
   notification of a $199 cruise. We have also taken

advantage of their deals for a sweet experience in Ireland ($1,199 covered two round-trip tickets, five nights at bed-and-breakfasts, and a rental car) and "honey time" in Hawaii ($799 covered airfare for two and five nights on Waikiki Beach).

⌘ Consider relocation cruises. If you don't want to sit and wait for the "Top 20," do your own research (Google "relocation cruises"). These special deals are offered when a ship is moving to a different port for a new assignment. For example, if the ship is relocating from the U.S. to Europe to be put into service for a Mediterranean cruise, it will take passengers for the ten-day journey and then you fly home. The rub is that you'll pay more than $199, and you'll usually pay for a one-way ticket as well, but you can still find fabulous deals.

⌘ Just say no. This little tip will save you hundreds of greenbacks. Closely evaluate all the specials offered on ship. You might as well call these specials "money-makers for the cruise line"; they offer art, jewelry, alcohol, and spa services as soon as you get on board. For example, you can sign up the first day for spa specials, but is it really a good deal to have a $239 stone massage for only $199? No. Instead, I chose the $99 Ladies Night Out special, where I received five fifteen-minute spa services (a facial, massage, and hair treatment). Say no to spa extras, special drinks, jewelry (which will likely be on sale for 50 percent off the last day of the cruise), photos, and more.

⌘ Pass on the soda. The first day you may be offered a "soda pass" that gives you all the pop you can drink

for one low price. *Au contraire!* You want to drink
lots of *water, not soda,* on this cruise to get your
money's worth. Water keeps you hydrated after all the
salt in that rich food. Plus, you might feel obligated to
drink your weight in soda if you buy a pass, and the
end result will be an unhealthy feeling (even with diet
soda). The goal isn't to leave the cruise feeling bloated
and stressed but healthy and relaxed instead.

- Pack two water bottles. Each person should pack two
  bottles of water (we stick them in shoes in our lug-
  gage) to save big bucks. You cannot bring in cases of
  water or six-packs of soda. That's generally not allowed. Water onboard sells for $2.50 to $4.00 per
  bottle, and it also costs that much onshore too. But
  you can bring a couple of bottles to use and refill.
  The tap water in your room is usually the same
  water source used for glasses of water in the dining
  room. Keep and refill your bottles (while on board,
  not on land) to save on the cost of having to buy
  new bottles at ports of call and while on excursions.

- Don't forget your camera! One of my fave nights is
  formal night, and photos are a must. By all means
  take photos from the ship's service. You can look at
  them later and don't have to buy them. But be sure
  to have your new friends on board take plenty of
  digital pictures with your own camera—you'll save
  the cost of the formal photo and probably get better
  shots.

- Rank and research shore excursions. You could easily
  double or triple the bottom-line cost for your cruise
  by spending money on shore excursions. Before you

sail, when you go to the cruise Web site to print your boarding pass, look at the shore excursions and print out the options. Or do this as soon as you get aboard. You and your sailing mate (spouse, friend, child, mom) should rank the excursions. The first step is to pick the ones you *like best* for each port. Then both of you can pick your top three for each port of call, giving a number three to your top pick, two for the second best, and one for your last choice. Give the same ranking for the excursion with the *most time* (for example, a five-hour island tour): three for the most time, two for the second most, one for the least amount of time. Finally, rank the cost of each: three for the least expensive, two for the next expensive, and one for the most money. Add up all of these, and the excursion with the biggest number is usually the best value.

⌗ Watch out for those excursion extras. Try to walk as much as possible on excursions and avoid bus, shuttle, or cab fares. It's important to walk and work off some of that rich food. You'll feel better and get more for your money, time, and effort. Bring your own water bottles (see earlier tip), and don't throw away the bottle when you're done. Eat breakfast on board before you go, to save money on food. Try to postpone lunch until you're back on the ship, or take an apple or banana to tide you over (we order room service the night before a port of call and have these delivered to our room). If the port is close to a town, you can even walk back on board (getting that coveted exercise), eat lunch, and then go back out again.

Did You Know?

Cruise line spas make most of their money by selling products to the relaxed and unaware. Yes, they make most of their money on the "necessities" they try to sell you. It's pretty amazing—the staff starts to sell while they're massaging your shoulders or finishing up your beautiful hair, while you're relaxed and vulnerable. Then they tell you how your hair is in really bad shape or your muscles need a special oil. In my hands-on research, I discovered that most cruise lines require their staff to pitch products. You can avoid the hard sell by saying something like, "You know, if you don't mind, I'd like just to relax in silence a while. I need the space." They'll understand, and you'll walk away with the relaxing knowledge of savvy savings.

Question:

I've seen those commercials about how much cheaper Priceline can be. But I've also heard you don't get a lot of choice. Is it really that great of a deal? And if so, what exactly can I expect once I try it out?

Answer:

Priceline does offer some great deals. It's unique from other auction sites because no one bids against you—they just let you know if you can have the price you bid. If you're going to use it, you will need to keep the following things in mind:

- Do your research on the lowest fare you can find and plan to bid about 20 percent lower than that fare. If you don't get the bid, you've lost nothing.
- Have your credit card ready.
- Enter your destination, departing and arrival airports, and dates of departure and arrival.
- Enter your price bid.
- Remember these are nonrefundable, and you cannot control the departure or arrival times.
- Usually within twenty-four hours you'll have an acceptance or rejection.
- If you are rejected, *you cannot enter the same information with a higher price!* You will have to change one of the pieces of information listed—departure or arrival airports or travel dates—and then make your bid again with a higher price.

So the catch is to look at all the options for arrivals and departures and bid on the most popular airports, most convenient departure and arrival times first, and save some other airports in the same vicinity as a backup in case they do not accept your price.

This system is good only if you have some flexibility in your schedule and know you won't need to make changes.

My friend Brenda Taylor had to drive fifty miles out of her way, leave on a date she didn't want to leave, and arrive later than intended just to save $50. Since she couldn't use the flight as a frequent-flier benefit on her usual airline, she decided it wasn't worth it.

On the other hand, our oldest daughter booked a flight from California to New York to see some friends for only $150. She booked it six months in advance, and it was truly worth the risk since inconvenience was a non-issue in her case.

8

Save Big on Gifts

12-Minute Tip #7: Layer the savings online and get as much as 50 percent off your gift purchases by following three steps: (1) comparison shop to get the best price with a shopping robot such as www.mysimon.com; (2) get free shipping, further discounts, and gifts for what you are buying by going to a code site such as www.dealhunting.com; (3) get an ebate (rebate) for items purchased by going to www.ebates.com. This takes an average of twelve minutes, and some of the families who are doing this have saved $1,200 per year on gifts alone!

Before we had kids of our own, I remember watching a very indulged little boy, who was around five years old, open present after present at his birthday party. Finally he grew tired and announced, "I'm done here. I'm going to go outside and swing!" I vowed that one day, when we had kids, we would simplify our holidays to the point that we didn't have to say "love and joy" through giving too many pricey gifts!

One area that can wreak havoc on your spending plan is gifts. Think about the presents you buy for relatives, baby showers, weddings, birthdays, Valentine's Day, Mother's

Day, Father's Day, kids' birthdays, and anniversaries. In the military we also have welcome gifts, farewells, pin-on's, hospitality, and the list goes on. And this doesn't even cover the biggie—Christmas.

For too many people, their *current* spending levels will eventually tire them out in the *future*—and not just in the obvious area of the holidays, but in *all* of gift giving. I know people who have given birthday presents that cost more than a week's salary. It's insane! Especially since a more realistic and doable amount of money to spend on gifts (all of them combined) is 2 percent of your monthly earnings.

If you tend to go a little—or a lot!—crazy when it comes to purchasing presents, you should be as wary of the temptation to overspend as the little boy was of opening too many presents.

Trust me, you can give amazing, astounding, awesome presents without spending amazing, astounding, awesomely high amounts of cash (or credit).

⤫

- ▦ Ask yourself, do you *really* have to give a material gift in every circumstance? Wouldn't a card work just as well in some cases? Or a personal letter that's filled with words of appreciation?
- ▦ Consider making or baking some of your gifts. I value handmade or homemade gifts, because I know the time and effort that goes into them. Most of my welcome and hospitality gifts are baked goods. I've yet to have someone turn up their nose at a hot loaf of honey wheat bread given as a hospitality present.

⌗ Watch for sales on trial-size products such as lotions and fragrance body washes. Then when you want to give an encouragement gift or something simple, arrange them in a basket with a loofah or put them in a gift bag.

⌗ Instead of buying gifts for Valentine's Day, Mother's Day, Father's Day, Groundhog Day, etc., issue a coupon book with homemade coupons for items your family members or friends truly enjoy. This little booklet has about ten coupons in it and requires plenty of forethought. They are gifts of time and love.

   One Mother's Day, my son Daniel gave me coupons for five free baby-sitting hours, my son Philip gave me a coupon for doing one of my chores, and my daughter Bethany gave me a coupon for a back rub. In return, Bob and I surprised them with coupon books of their own! We gave them each a coupon for a trip out with Mom or Dad for ice cream, one free bed-making day, a trip to the park, a candy bar of their choice, and their favorite breakfast for a day—I think you get the general idea. The key is individualizing the coupon book and taking the time to make it special.

⌗ Give the gift of a Facebook page for Mother's Day. Middle-aged women are the most quickly growing demographic on Facebook! Set it up and have the family write a profile for Mom. Tweens and teens love this one, and even Dad can get involved. Your mom can then use the site to do her own social and professional networking as well as to keep in touch with the family.

- ⌘ Help a family member, friend, or neighbor to organize a room. Many moms can feel frazzled because of disorganization. Give Mom a room of her choice and help her clean it out and simplify things. Design a gift certificate that's good for a few hours one morning or afternoon. From the kitchen to her office, this is a great idea for any home area that needs de-cluttering. She'll not only love the stress-busting effects of an organized environment, but even more importantly, the time she'll have with you. For more ideas on how to organize, go to Marcia Ramsland's site, www.organizingpro.com.

- ⌘ Assemble a playlist for your special someone's iPod or other portable music player. Know some songs that bring your someone special to mind? Nothing will bring a smile to his or her face faster than music with lyrics that say what that person means to you or that take him or her back to a special time. Think Bette Midler's "Wind Beneath My Wings" or the Caribbean tunes played on vacation.

- ⌘ Give a YouTube tribute. Take it one step further and marry one or two of her favorite tunes with photos and funny videos from the family collection for a full multimedia extravaganza. Post it at www.youtube.com. These can also be assembled into a special e-book online at www.snapfish.com.

- ⌘ Plant a vegetable garden. Stake out a piece of the backyard or fill window boxes, barrels and tubs, urns or pots, and hanging baskets with seedlings and starter plants for a vegetable and/or herb garden. Aside from the food bill savings, harvesting the bounty will provide months of good taste and good cheer.

Did You Know? ─────────────────────

Sometimes "hard times" bring back the good old days. In 2009, Americans spent 11 percent less on Mother's Day than they did in 2008.[1] Even so, moms still hauled away $9 billion in booty. While this may mean less money spent, it didn't mean that moms were neglected. In fact, more families were focusing on homemade dinners made by the family, handmade cards, a nature hike or boulevard stroll with kids, and plenty of conversation. So rather than looking at your favorite holiday as being more restrictive in difficult economic times, think outside your normal parameters and make it more creative and meaningful than ever.

CHRISTMAS

▦ Limit the number of gifts. One way our large family of seven holds debt at bay is to limit our giving to three gifts per person. We told the kids years ago that if three gifts were good enough for the baby Jesus, then three gifts were good enough for them. This tradition has helped to keep the focus on the season, where it belongs—in caring for each other and our community in a spirit of love and joy.

Sandy from Colorado started doing this. Here's the letter I received about her decision:

I wanted to try your Christmas simplification plan with the three gifts and didn't know how our family would take it. But our finances really needed it. It seems like it takes forever to pay off the credit card bills from Christmas. We explained the idea to the kids, and they seemed to understand. They even made a game of trying to pick three simple gifts they really wanted.

Well, it worked beautifully! We told the kids they may not get everything on their list and they understood. We were able to find a lot of gifts for them on clearance that they liked even better than the original items on their list! For the first time in seven years, we do not have credit card bills to pay off after our Christmas shopping. The emphasis this year was on the reason for the season, and we don't have the headaches of bills to pay. Why didn't we start this system years ago?

⌗ Start early and purchase gifts all year long. Shop the clearance aisles and loss leaders. These expenses can be absorbed into your monthly budget, and you get the benefit of sales and clearance prices on gifts. When a good deal shows up on sale, buy it and keep it in a safe place. I know a father of eight who starts buying Christmas gifts in January. Every month he buys for one of his children. That way, once December rolls around, he doesn't have the stress of last-minute shopping and hasn't broken his bank account.

⌗ Use the above tip for more generic presents to keep on hand so that if a surprise guest shows up at your house, you'll have something to give. Make sure the gifts appeal to a broad range of tastes, such as holiday music or classic holiday DVDs like *It's a Wonderful Life* or *White Christmas*. Other safe gifts include holiday fashion accessories—from cuff links to earrings to socks and scarves.

⌗ Strategize on Black Friday. The day after Thanksgiving is the biggest shopping day of the year and it comes complete with loads of loss leaders (items stores sell at less than cost in order to lure you into their stores). Get your holiday ads on that Thursday and mark down all the sales you want to take advantage of. Map out a time frame of when to hit the stores that open first and then the stores that open later. If you have a shopping buddy, one can run for the discounted digital cameras while the other loads up on portable DVD players. Be sure to stick to your list and not give in to impulse buying and you'll come out strategically ahead of the average holiday shopper!

⌗ Document your purchases. There's nothing like buying Christmas paper to wrap those presents early only to discover a month later that you have tons of paper you bought at the end-of-season clearance last year that you forgot about. Or you get a good deal on gifts for friends, teachers, or neighbors, and then realize you bought those earlier in the year and forgot where you put them. To avoid the stress of forgetfulness and to save money by not overpurchasing items, write down your purchases—and where they're stored—on a piece of paper and tape it to

your December calendar page (but don't let your
kids see that page!).

✂ Be creative! By preparing homemade goods, such as
jams and jellies when the fruit is in season, you can
save a lot of money. Present your yummy gifts in
interesting baskets, boxes, tins, or other containers
you've found at garage sales or on clearance shelves.

✂ Give gift certificates. If you want to send an online
gift certificate to someone, it's as easy as pointing
and clicking. The recipient will receive notification
in his or her inbox that you've bought a gift certificate, and you can follow up with an e-card alerting
that person that the notification he or she will receive from the retailer is not spam. For some great
options, go to www.restaurant.com for discounts on
eating out or check out potential deals at www.fat
wallet.com. For a review of codes that can give you
a better deal, go to www.couponcabin.com or
www.dealhunting.com.

One warning: with all the recent store closings,
you really have to be cautious in buying gift cards,
because when a store files for bankruptcy or closes,
it's up to the bankruptcy courts to determine
whether or not the store has to honor the existing
gift cards. All too often, they don't have to. Some
closed stores are walking away from 20 million dollars in unhonored cards!

So if you want the convenience and portability
of a gift card, then stick to the prepaid credit cards
(Visa is a common one that I use for my college
kids) or a major store that ain't gonna ever close. In

fact, some families may appreciate a card to a major discount retailer because it will allow them to buy groceries and clothing without having you, the giver, go to the additional expense of what a prepaid Visa card costs.

- ⚏ Be organized. Marcia Ramsland wrote a great book called *Simplify the Holidays* that offers advice on how to strategize and simplify. This three-year planner advises you that getting organized can save you big bucks, and staying organized can save your sanity. Sounds like another good reason to simplify!

- ⚏ Wrap each present as you get it. Don't forget to label to whom each gift is intended. Once again, you may want to keep a master list of the gifts, listing the contents and numbering them as you buy them. That way you won't duplicate gifts or overbuy for any one person.

- ⚏ Decorate early. Decorate the weekend after Thanksgiving and you'll save money. By organizing all the Christmas decorations, you'll discover which items you need and which ones you do not need. Then you can look for those lights that are on sale to replace the ones that didn't survive last year. You also will not duplicate items that you bought on clearance the previous year. With your home decorated early, you'll be less likely to impulse-buy holiday decorations, and you won't have the job of decorating on your to-do list.

- ⚏ Buy Christmas paper, bows, cards, decorations, and nonperishable gifts on December 26. Think about those items that will store well and invest accord-

ingly. One season I bought enough (incredibly cute)
gift bags (at 90 percent off retail) to last five years!
My entire bag investment was only $10.

⚏ Sometimes the gift of time is the greatest gift of all
during the holidays. There are a number of ways you
can brighten the holidays of those around you and
share the season. Invite the family of a deployed military member over for the holiday dinner—these can
be the most difficult times of the year for people
who are separated from loved ones. If you are a
military family, participate in your on-base holiday
cookie drive. One year, our military base collected
120,000 cookies and distributed them to police offi-
cers, firefighters, and others who worked the holiday
shift. Check out my book *Living Rich for Less* for
other ways to share your blessings during the holidays and throughout the year.

Did You Know?

*The average American family takes until May of the
following year to pay off their Christmas charges. That
doesn't leave much money for vacations or to service
other debt.*

❧

Question:

Every Christmas my husband throws our budget out the
window and spends hundreds of dollars on presents for

our family and friends and co-workers and neighbors and church members. When I try to explain that we don't have that kind of money, he says, "But it's Christmas!" as though that's explanation enough for our overspending. What can I do?

Answer:

I can understand how this is a problem that can lead to arguments at Christmastime, and that's certainly not what Christmas is about! I would suggest you sit down with your husband and ask him about his definition of Christmas. You can do the same and compare notes. Then divide the list into two sections: the material and the nonmaterial. You'll find things like "presents, trees, decorations, hot cocoa" on the material side and items such as "love, peace, family, time spent together, goodwill toward others, etc." on the nonmaterial side. Then ask your husband, "What do you think our friends and family will remember from this list twenty years from now?" I think he'll find his answer: it's not the gifts that make the holiday special, it's the meaningful time spent with friends and family.

The final step is to make a commitment to each other that since Christmas is *not* about spending money and going further into debt, you'll set a financial plan and stick to it. You'll also set up practical ways to concentrate on making the nonmaterial side of the list more of a priority in your holidays.

9

Save Big on Medical, Dental, and Insurance

12-Minute Tip #8: Switch healthy family members off of the pricey group medical plan to a high deductible HSA (Health Savings Account) plan not only to save an average of $250 per month for a family of four, but also to build a supplemental retirement plan in the tax-favored HSA account. Take twelve minutes to get competitive quotes at www.ehealthinsurance.com and save $1,200 or more this year.

A year ago, I fell off a three-foot platform while speaking to a packed audience. Yep. There was an optical illusion on the stairs, and after my grand "performance," the usual speaker for that facility told me, "Wow, I've been worried about doing that myself for years. It's so hard to see those stairs!"

I thought, *Well, ya think ya coulda warned me about it?*

Fortunately, I didn't break any bones, but the trauma triggered a frozen shoulder and all kinds of nonsense: MRIs, x-rays, surgeon consults, and on and on. It's taken a year to recover. Puhleeze no "how could you fall for that?" jokes. Okay? I'm just glad I had insurance!

According to the Healthcare Cost and Utilization Project, if you or someone you love broke a leg, you would incur costs in excess of $15,000. It's no wonder that in my experience with American families, I've found that the greatest financial concern they have is how to find affordable health insurance.

Unfortunately, many families are misled in this area—they're sold a Rolls-Royce when a Ford will do just as well. You should consider spending about 5 percent of your monthly income on insurance (this includes health, life, auto, and home) and 4 percent on saving for medical and dental expenses.

Insurance, in general, is a supplementary provision for the family. It's not complete protection, and with the exception of Health Savings Accounts, you should not view it as a profit-making tool. If your agent is selling you a life insurance plan that is designed to be a savings account, then you need to reconsider that particular plan. My view is that life insurance policies should not be purchased as a retirement pad. These are costly mistakes made by people who are misinformed.

Even with the best insurance, though, it's not going to cover all your medical and dental expenses. So the following tips are easy, painless ways to trim the insurance, medical, and dental fat. They'll help you spend less money while making sure you have adequate coverage and care. These tips will give you confidence the next time you fall ☺ so that you can get up again and keep going!

❧

MEDICAL

- ❦ The best protection against rising medical costs is still prevention. First Place (www.firstplace.org) and Weight Watchers (www.weightwatchers.com) are fabulous health programs for men and women of all ages. Using a support system that incorporates balanced eating and exercise plans, these groups provide the accountability and opportunity to change your life. A healthy lifestyle can also have other advantages. Many health insurance companies offer a refund on an annual premium if the insured can prove that they have attended a health and fitness center three times a week or by being a member of Weight Watchers.

- ❦ Make friends with your doctor. Take him or her oatmeal cookies and milk. Find someone you can trust before you need him or her.

- ❦ Choose a doctor who believes in preventive medicine. I have a holistic doctor that I see in addition to our general practice physician—a second, more natural opinion just makes me better informed.

- ❦ Find a doctor who will answer minor health questions over the phone. When searching for a physician, let them know this point is important to you and will help determine who you see as your family's doctor. Believe it or not, doctors also feel the pinch when the economy turns down. People don't visit them as often for minor ailments, and consequently their revenues may be down.

- ❦ Follow your doctor's prescription. For example, dietary restrictions or taking antibiotics.

⊞ When selecting a hospital, shop around—not all hospitals charge the same.

⊞ Ask for an itemized hospital bill and review it for duplicate or erroneous charges. I once found five entries on my bill for services they routinely performed for women in my situation (birthing a baby) but did not perform for me because I had my baby three minutes after we arrived at the hospital (while Bob was parking the car).

⊞ Ask for routine tests to be done before hospital admission. You can save significantly, since hospitals can sometimes charge as much as double or more.

⊞ If you have to have surgery, ask your doctor if day surgery is a possibility. Outpatient surgery does not require an overnight hospital stay and could lower your bills quite a bit. The only exception would be the terms of your insurance provider and if an overnight stay is required in order to cover the procedure. So check with your provider first and then make an informed decision.

⊞ Get a second opinion for surgery, and ask for a referral from the primary physician before you get the second opinion so that it will be covered by your insurance policy.

⊞ Question your doctor (your friend) in advance about medical costs. Although he or she cannot influence the amount the hospital or the anesthesiologist charges you, you would be surprised at how much latitude doctors have in what they charge for their own services.

⚎ Go to www.webmd.com or another reputable site to educate yourself about medical issues to determine the value of the care you receive.

⚎ Shop around for prescriptions, taking advantage of transfer specials—and coupons! We routinely get a $20 gift card for transferring our prescription to another store we visit on a regular basis.

⚎ Ask about cash discounts for prescriptions.

⚎ Take advantage of the lower priced medications. You can check online at your pharmacy's Web site to see the list of $4 medications.

⚎ Routinely ask for the generic version of your prescription; this can save as much as half the cost in some cases.

⚎ Most of us know that we should eliminate the following from our lifestyles:
  • smoking
  • alcohol
  • fatty foods
  • sugars

  But it's oftentimes difficult to succeed in these areas. You might want to consider joining an accountability group such as Weight Watchers or an "overcomers" group at your local church that specializes in all kinds of addictions. Studies indicate that people are more likely to find success in a supportive group than by going it alone.

⚎ Drink plenty of water (eight 8-ounce glasses a day is ideal).

⚎ Maintain a positive attitude and evaluate those around you who are positive and negative. I've had to minimize my time around pessimists or I find myself in the grumps on a regular basis! Although sometimes my Little Miss Sunshine friends are *sooo* optimistic that I feel the spirit of slap come over me—especially if I'm tired. So there's a balance, but I'd rather err on the positive side!

⚅ Get a physical checkup at least once every three years, more often if you are over fifty.

⚅ Get children's shots at the county health office or find another resource for inexpensive or free shot clinics at www.ehealthinsurance.org.

⚅ Ask your doctor for free samples of your needed medication.

Did You Know?

If you worry about using generic brands of medications versus the name-brand version because the generic brand may not be as effective, worry no more. The Food and Drug Administration (FDA) requires the same active ingredient in the generics as in the regular, more expensive brands.

DENTAL

⚅ Teach your children to brush their teeth and floss properly. And while you're at it, make sure you model for them by doing your own! I take portable, disposable flossers and use them while reading in bed or watching a movie with the kids. In fact, after we saw some of the character's teeth in *Pirates of the Caribbean,* I passed them out for the whole family and they took them willingly!

⌗ Schedule regular dental checkups for every member of your family and ask your dentist's office to send you regular reminder cards.

⌗ Get a second opinion for extensive dental work.

Did You Know?

You can negotiate a dental bill even after the service has been rendered. When you get the balance-due bill, make a twelve-minute phone call to the office and ask them (respectfully) if there's anything they can do about this bill. Most clinics understand difficult economic times, and while you don't have to go into a long sob story, you can tell them that times are difficult and it would be wonderful if you could find some relief from even a portion of the bill. Readers have responded to me with their inspiring success stories. Just mind your Ps: be prepared (know what you owe and when it's due), be polite (you catch more flies with honey than vinegar), and be persistent (if the answer is no, ask to speak to a supervisor or go directly to the dentist).

HEALTH INSURANCE

⌗ The best and least expensive medical insurance you can have is probably the plan your employer provides, *especially if they pay your premium.* This is usually a group policy offering group rates for dependents. Check into the monthly fees you pay and the coverage you receive in your group plan so you can shop around for a competitive price. Some group rates may require that you buy their life insurance policy and may add administrative fees per person. Be sure you get the total costs so you can comparison shop armed with accurate information.

🎏 Medical insurance should be a provision for major medical expenses. A medical plan is not primarily designed to cover Joshua's trip to the doctor for a runny nose or Daniel's strep throat. We can cover those out of pocket if we have to do so in order to make sure we have the big things covered. A good health insurance plan should cover 80 percent of the medical bills in the event of a major illness.

🎏 If you have to buy your own insurance, go to the library first and look at *Best's Insurance Reports* to find an A-rated company whose specialty is health care. You can also view this report online, but it is a product to buy and costs anywhere from $1,300 to $1,995! Some self-employed people use Golden Rule (www.goldenrule.com), now a part of United Healthcare as an option. Consider raising your major medical deductible to $1,000—since the majority of the premium goes to cover the first $1,000. Try to make sure your plan has a no-deductible accident provision. You may also want to find a plan that will pay for a second opinion if your physician advises surgery.

🎏 There's no need to pay more than necessary for health insurance. Compare plans and prices by going to a nonintrusive site such as www.ehealth

insurance.com. It's possible to get a relatively anonymous quote instantly without the intrusion of a salesperson calling your home or office. It's also a good place to compare plans by remembering that you shouldn't buy what you don't need. For example, if you do not need maternity benefits, eliminate them from the plan you choose.

⚞ Ideally, it would be best if you could consider a higher deductible. Then the money saved on premiums could go into a Health Savings Account (HSA), which is basically a health insurance policy you can bank on. (For more in-depth information about an HSA, see my book *Living Rich for Less*.) When you purchase an HSA-eligible policy in conjunction with an HSA account, the Health Savings Account is funded with pre-tax dollars, and your taxable income is reduced at the same time. You can use the money in this account tax-free to fund healthcare-related costs, including prescriptions, doctor's visits, insurance deductibles, and over-the-counter medications. Then what you don't spend can be rolled over from year to year and can serve as an eventual supplement to your existing retirement plan.

One important footnote is that you must establish an HSA before incurring any expenses, or the expenses will not qualify.

For a complete list of HSA eligible plans or to investigate signing up for one of these savings accounts, go to www.ehealthinsurance.com. Since the funds you put into this account are carried over each year, the worst-case scenario is that you remain healthy and use the HSA very little. In which case you'd have more money in that account growing tax-free until you're sixty-five years old, and then you can withdraw it without paying taxes. Sounds like a win-win deal to me!

⌘ Never buy two primary policies on one person (you could buy a primary and a supplemental, however). If you purchase two primary policies, you pay twice, but you can't collect twice! And if you do plan on collecting twice, then I hear they have free medical care in your local jail because it's considered a scam. If you are currently covered under your employer's plan and have family members covered under that group policy, then consider moving your spouse (and kids) into an individual health insurance plan instead. By pulling them out of pricey group plans, you could save your family as much as $2,500 per year.

Make sure the individual policies will allow you to add yourself if your company's group plan benefits go away because of the economy or if your company downsizes and you are out of work. The only time you would not want to do this is if family members have preexisting conditions (like asthma, diabetes, etc.), and you do not want it excluded from the individual policy. In that case, it would be better to pay the higher premium in a group plan in order to keep the comprehensive coverage consistent. Otherwise, you can save hundreds each month by using the benefits of an individual policy. The exception to this rule is found in states that require all health insurance providers to cover all preexisting conditions. Check with your provider to see the rules that govern your state's health insurance requirements.

- Remember that there is no need for an "all or nothing" approach to health insurance. If you have a family member with a preexisting condition, then enroll them on your employer's group policy and let the other family members go with an individual policy. By dividing your coverage among a couple of different plans, you are paying the least price possible for the most coverage and still getting each family member on a plan of some kind.

- Don't cancel an existing policy until you have new coverage in place and have completed any waiting period; you don't want a gap in your coverage.

- Know the difference between health insurance and discount health or medical "cards." According to the Coalition Against Insurance Fraud (CAIF), many companies are selling so-called discount health cards to consumers seeking affordable healthcare. For a monthly fee, the cards claim to save subscribers money by offering discounts on physician visits, hospital stays, prescription drugs, dental work, eye care, and other treatment. CAIF says, "Discount health cards are spreading rapidly. Many may offer valuable, money-saving benefits for people without health insurance. But these cards can also be confusing because they are not insurance. You still must pay the medical bills yourself. These cards simply offer lower prices on services that accept these discounts."[1] If you have a question about a policy or a card before you buy, go to www.insurancefraud.org to make sure you're being wise in your choices and you're getting what you think you're paying for in that card.

▦ Budget for COBRA (Consolidated Omnibus Budget Reconciliation Act). If the rumor mill at work is buzzing that health insurance benefits will be cut, start setting aside money for COBRA, a health insurance that remains in effect even if you lose benefits or your job. This benefit will allow you to keep the current group policy for up to eighteen months— but it's pricey. I recommend that you set up an allotment from your paycheck and start putting a little extra each month into a savings account especially set up for this purpose. This method of recession-proofing your insurance needs will help tide you over between insurance providers in the event these benefits go away. Go to www.cobrahealth.com for more details.

▦ If you're one of the 45.8 million uninsured Americans who may feel they cannot afford health insurance, go to the nonprofit arm at www.ehealth insurance.org to see what services and benefits are available for your particular situation and in your state and community.

Did You Know?

Taking care of yourself, exercising regularly, and maintaining a decent weight is the best insurance against medical costs. Get regular checkups and teach your children good health habits. Smoking and excessive drinking are both habits that will cost you plenty in the long run.

LIFE INSURANCE

✂ The basic principle to remember in life insurance is to purchase insurance for *provision* and not *investment*. Therefore, term insurance is cheaper and more affordable. However, you need to evaluate your family's needs and make your decision accordingly. You want your family to be provided for in the event of your death—not benefit from your death. To determine how much life insurance you need if your survivors invest the life insurance benefits they receive, go to my Web site, www.elliekay.com, click on Tool Center, and check out the Life Insurance Need Calculator.

✂ The need for life insurance diminishes with age. Term insurance is still available up to the age of sixty-five or seventy. However, a seventy-year-old shouldn't have the dependents and the debt of a thirty-year-old and will, therefore, require less life insurance.

✂ If you currently have a whole life policy, have your agent reevaluate your program. You may want to convert it to term or borrow the cash reserve and invest it in a program with a higher interest rate. For insurance quotes, call Select Quote at 1-800-343-1985 or Insure.com at 1-800-431-1147. Or go to www.selectquote.com. or www.insure.com.

✂ Reconsider any life insurance on your children. If the purpose of life insurance is to *provide* and not *invest,* then why do we need life insurance on children? Some misguided parents have life insurance programs on their children as investment programs for college—this is not a financially wise decision! Life insurance on children should cover only funeral expenses.

Did You Know?

I used to be an insurance broker, and if I have to generalize, I'd say insurance brokers are good people doing an honest job. However, the way the system works is that some life insurance brokers make as much as 50 percent of the premiums you pay for the first year you have certain policies. Consequently, they may direct you to a policy that has higher premiums, which may also have a higher commission. This is also true of some health insurance policies. So make sure you do your own research on any kind of recommended policy by following the simple tips I've outlined in this section and in my book Living Rich for Less. *Then spend that extra money on building your own vacation savings account rather than paying for your broker's new Jet Ski and matching Speedo.*

❧

Question:

I can't keep track of all the different types of life insurance. How do I know what would be best for me?

Answer:

There are many kinds of life insurance plans on the market. You almost need to go to school to understand them—

or so it seems. Basically, life insurance can be divided into two categories: term and permanent or whole life. Talk to your insurance agent about the difference between the policies available and what's best for you and your family. Ask about the differences between these types of life insurance: level term, whole life, universal life, variable life, annual renewable term, and variable universal life (permanent). Or see the chart "Everything You Wanted to Know About Life Insurance" in my book *Living Rich for Less*.

10

Save Big on Furniture and Appliances

12-Minute Tip #9: Go to your local furniture store and select the style/model that you like, then take that info back home and search for the best price on the Internet by going to search sites such as www .fatwallet.com. Take the best price back to the store and ask them to match it. One family took twelve minutes to do their research and saved $1,200 on chairs for a new dining room set.

Even though I've got a little pioneer blood running through my veins, I wouldn't want to live in the pioneer days—I'd miss my dishwasher too much. When you read accounts of nineteenth- and twentieth-century living, you'll notice that most upper-class and even many middle-class people employed a servant or two. These domestic employees often boarded in the home and cooked, washed dishes and clothes, purchased food every day, and served the family in their daily life. I could use a few full-time domestic employees! But in one way, I already have a few.

Today we have servants too. They are called "appliances." They cook our food (oven, stove, microwave, slow cooker, toaster oven), preserve our food (refrigerator and freezer), prepare our food (mixer, blender, dehydrator, pasta maker, juicer), and dispose of our food (garbage disposal, trash compactor). These servants wash our dishes (dishwasher, Daniel, Philip), wash and dry our clothes (washer and dryer), and clean our carpets (vacuum cleaner, Bethany, and rug shampooer). They take care of our hair (blow-dryers, curlers, and curling irons), pretty up our faces (shavers, makeup mirrors, and electric tweezers), and pamper our bodies (foot massagers—yea!). I'm sure you could add to this list, and I believe you get the point. Appliances are modern-day servants.

These domestic employee equivalents make our lives easier on one condition—we must take care of them. None of these servants earn their keep if they aren't working, so maintenance is important and can save us hundreds of dollars. Servants not only need to work well, they also vary in cost and effectiveness. The following tips are designed to help you find, buy, maintain, and appreciate the domestic servants you keep at home.

⌘ As you prepare for these high-priced purchases, the first thing to do is to take inventory.

Ask yourself three questions when you are considering major purchases:

- Do I need it?
- Can I afford it?
- How am I going to pay for it?

I'll give you a hint on the answers to the above questions, they should be "yes," followed by a "yes," and then "cash, not credit."

⌗ Set aside an emergency fund with as little as 1 percent of your monthly income—building the fund to a healthy amount. When you need to replace something, you'll have the cash and won't spend more by using credit. To save the most on furniture and appliances, the smart thing to do is to prepare for these purchases *before* you need to make them. If you wait until the washing machine goes completely out before you think about the possibility of having to purchase another one, you could spend up to 50 percent more by not having the time to shop for the best value and by being forced to buy it on credit!

FURNITURE

⌗ Write down your dream list and take it to a furniture store. The sticker shock, or the price of the furniture you just can't live without, may force you to reassess your furniture needs.

⌗ Evaluate your genuine furniture needs. Can you recover that couch with fabric from a wholesaler? Can you buy a slipcover for that chair? Does your mom have a piece of furniture or an appliance sitting in her storage shed that you could use?

⌗ To significantly increase the life of your furniture and to save the upholstery, try these ideas:

- Throw a nice looking afghan on the back of your couch or on your recliner.
- Use the armchair covers that come with your couches or wing chairs in order to prevent wear on the highly used parts of the furniture.

⚅ Before discarding old furniture or an appliance to get a new one, get an estimate on a complete overhaul. Or better yet, can you repair or rebuild that couch with a fix-it guide? Perhaps you can learn to reupholster and varnish as a new family hobby. Your local community college or county extension office may even offer classes on these skills.

⚅ Reupholster your furniture. You can find some great upholstery fabric values on the Internet by searching the manufacturer.

⚅ Often the brochures offered at the furniture store will have a Web site for the manufacturer. Do a little research online at the manufacturer's site to find an outlet store link. Search for the price (including shipping and handling), availability, and delivery of the furniture you want. Then print out those prices and take them back to your local store to give them an opportunity to match the competition's price.

⚅ Explore the manufacturer's site and request a list of all the distributors of the brand-name furniture in a hundred-mile radius. Printing the price list and making a few calls to the stores in your area could save you as much as 50 percent on your choices. Be sure to show your sales resistance when you call the local stores for a price check, and don't forget to ask them if they can beat the deal you have by throwing in free delivery, a free fabric guard treatment, or any other freebie. So often these items are yours for the asking.

⚅ Consider vintage furniture. This is furniture built several decades ago that isn't old enough to qualify as antique. These pieces make for remarkable values because the craftsmanship is often superior to furniture built today. You can find them typically at estate sales, garage sales, auctions, or secondhand furniture stores. Before you buy, turn the item over and look at the joints to see if they're in solid shape.

If you're looking for a couch, research in advance the cost of fabric and labor for reupholstering. For example, we found fabric at an outlet store for only $3/yard. The same fabric at the furniture store was $38/yard. We also knew in advance how much it would cost for labor to reupholster our couch and love seat. In the end, we saved 40 percent for the style of our choice using this approach.

- When purchasing baby furniture, ask yourself, "Is this for our first child, and do we plan on having more?" You may do well to buy new and consider it an investment if this is your first child. If this is a late-in-your-life baby or a "one is enough" child, then all you need is a nice-looking, used crib to make it through one baby.

- If you plan on three or more years between children, then consider a crib that will convert to a youth bed.

- Buy a display model. Most merchandisers sell their display models at a considerable discount.

APPLIANCES

- Purchase your small appliances from garage sales. Much of what we think we *need* is simply what we *want*. Do you really need all those little appliances that take up so much room and perform such a lim-

---

Did You Know?

You should never buy furniture on credit without taking a look at the total price you'll end up paying for the purchase. The "steal" of a love seat that costs $500 will end up costing you an amazing $1,200 after several years on a low-payment, high-interest-rate schedule. If you're buying several pieces of furniture, you could accumulate $10,000 in credit card debt for furniture alone. By making only the minimum payment on that loan, at 18 to 22 percent interest, it will take you more than thirty-three years and $26,000 to pay it off. Count the cost before you buy to avoid the endless cycle of debt.

---

ited function? Go to garage sales, and you'll see all the stuff folks can do without. There you can buy your juicer, dehydrator, pasta maker, bagel baker, jerky jerker, taffy puller, and…well, I think you get the idea.

- Check out secondhand stores, garage sales, and classifieds. We purchased a used Maytag washer and dryer and had them for more than thirteen years and twelve thousand loads of laundry. We only had to replace a timing chain and another part damaged in a move—but the $500 we invested in them was money well spent.

- Appliances that are removed from the box and used as store displays usually sell at discounted rates. By buying a store display and taking advantage of the reduced price and/or a rebate, you can save major dollars. The guarantee is usually the same as any other new appliance in a box. Call around to your local dealers and ask for these values.

⚏ Don't waste precious dollars on extended warranties; instead, use the kind of credit card that offers to automatically double the manufacturer's warranty and then pay off the balance the next month. Some gold cards offer this double warranty option, so call your credit card company to make sure your card has this benefit.

⚏ Sometimes searching the Internet can work well for appliances to get a price comparison that you can take to your local dealer and ask them to match. Remember, though, that shipping and handling add up on larger appliances. Still, this method is highly effective in getting a better price from your local dealer.

⚏ A rather unconventional, yet highly effective way to find serviceable merchandise is to advertise what you need on a bulletin board—or check out the posted items to find out what is available. These bulletin boards can be found in grocery stores, churches, military family support centers, breakrooms in places of employment, libraries, and many other places, including Craigslist online or the online classifieds from your local newspaper.

⚏ Pick up a copy of the current *Consumer Reports Buying Guide* at your library to check out the appliance or furniture you need. Then armed with that research, shop the sales at each store. Compare warranties, delivery charges, and features.

🔳 Avoid deluxe models—they have too many extra bells and whistles. You don't need them. We bought a small freezer and saved 35 percent by eliminating two unnecessary features—the equivalent of one bell and one whistle!

🔳 Look at discontinued furniture and last year's models.

🔳 Ask the salesperson when the item might go on sale. If you just missed a sale by a couple of weeks, ask the manager for the previous sale price. Often you "have not because you ask not."

┌─ *Did You Know?* ─────────────────────────

Wise shoppers can save hundreds of dollars each year in a minimal amount of time by simply doing their homework.

└──┘

∾

Question:

Some friends of ours have beautiful handmade furniture from a local craftsman. I'm so jealous, but my family and I are on a tight budget. How can I get furniture like theirs—or at least not obsess about it?

Answer:

It may surprise you to find out that *some* craftsmen can build a custom-made dining room set for less than the best sale price of a comparable quality set at a traditional store. (We're talking quality furniture here—not sale items from the local discount department store.) To locate a craftsman in your area, call the local lumberyard, antique store, or furniture repair shop for recommendations. Or Google or look in the Yellow Pages under Furniture Designers and Custom Builders.

Don't waste their time or yours when you call for an estimate. Decide the following before you call: (1) the style of furniture and how many pieces, (2) the type and quality of wood, (3) whether you want paint, varnish, or bare wood, (4) the fabric design and/or pattern, and (5) your price range. Be flexible in exploring "wants" versus "needs" in the pieces you would like to order. Ask the right questions, such as:

"May I see samples of your work and references?"

"Do you guarantee the pieces?"

"What is the estimated delivery time on the work?"

"If I order several rooms' worth of furniture, what percentage discount could you give me?"

"How long have you been building furniture?"

You may even consider asking, "Is there a less expensive style or way to build this piece that will make it more affordable for our family?"

A reputable craftsman will not be offended by these practical questions and should be willing to stand behind his or her work. The end result could be lovely, custom-made furniture that can be passed on to the next generation and something you'll be thrilled to show off to your friends!

11

Save Big on Education

Our daughter Bethany went back to school this semester, but about 15 percent of her classmates did not. It's the latest phenomenon in my kids' colleges (did I mention I have *three* in college at once?). Students are returning home because parents cannot afford to keep them in school. Many parents who relied on refinancing their home mortgage or a HELOC (Home Equity Line of Credit) are finding that they are upside down in their mortgages and there's no room to spare.

When people ask me how we are putting our kids

through college debt free, the answer is multifold. First, we train our children from a young age that going to school, doing your homework, and getting good grades is their primary job. By teaching them a good work ethic, we are laying the groundwork for scholarships and more. Second, we send them to schools that we can afford or where they get the best scholarship offers to cover the most expenses. Third, we have saved a modest amount of college money to help them pay their room and board and partial tuition. Last but certainly not least, we require that they work part time in the summers or during the school year (through a work-study program or a regular job) in order to do their part in paying for college. By implementing these four disciplines, each of our children is set to graduate debt free. Of the three who are going to college now, we have more than half a million dollars in scholarships, and if the last two stay true to their goals, our kids will have garnered more than a million dollars in scholarships by the time they graduate.

While an average of 40 percent of students who attend college get financial aid, grants, or scholarships, this only averages out to assistance of $9,600 per year. This leaves a boatload that the student and Mom/Dad owe for college. Most of this is usually in loans of some kind. If you want to get a good idea of the kind of money you'll need for college, go to the Tool Center at www.elliekay.com and click on the College Funding Calculator.

While in *Living Rich for Less* I cover extensively the topic of education, in this chapter we'll discuss some tips to help put college in perspective and some ways to get that education without hocking your future to do so. We've used several of these for our kids, and every thousand dollars we *don't* have to spend on tuition, college credits, books, or room and board is a thousand dollars that will counter the huge student loan debt that most parents assume as par for the education course.

~

SAVINGS PHILOSOPHIES

▣ One of the best things you can do for your college fund is to teach your kids a good work ethic at home and at school. Ride the homework train with them in the afternoons. Teach them that getting good grades; pursuing passions in sports, academics, and the arts; and working hard are their main jobs throughout school. And be sure to let them know that you expect them not only to get scholarships but also to participate in work-study programs, have jobs in the summer, or otherwise actually earn part of their way through school!

▣ Instead of asking, "What college did my child get accepted into?" ask, "What college did my child get accepted into that he or she can afford?" Adopt the philosophy that you'll send your child to the best school they can get accepted into that you can afford. Go to www.myplan.com and check out the Career Colleges database, which provides detailed profiles on more than 4,200 vocational schools in the United States.

▣ Start early. It's wise to start putting away money for college early—while they're still babies. You may want to start a custodial account at your bank. These are irrevocable gifts to the child and up to $700 per year of the investment income is tax-free. Once the fund has grown beyond $10,000, you're probably better off putting additional capital in either an education IRA or one of two state tuition programs.

Did You Know?

Every year, millions of parents make the devastating financial choice to give up their retirement investments to pay for their children's college. Do not be one of those parents! Your college funding plan should not include anything close to a home equity loan, a HELOC (home equity line of credit), or refinancing of an existing home mortgage.

These options reduce the amount of equity in your home, increasing the risk of possible foreclosure, and you incur costs in interest charges that may cost you more if the term on the new mortgage is greater than the remaining term on the existing mortgage. For example, if there are ten years left on the mortgage and parents get a new thirty-year loan. Some parents even choose to pull out enough money in equity for all four years of college at once. Those parents pay interest on money that their children won't need until the upcoming sophomore, junior, and senior years.

HIGH SCHOOL OPTIONS

⌗ See if your children can take advanced placement (AP) and international baccalaureate (IB) classes in high

school. Several of our kids have taken these classes
throughout their high school years. These are college-
level courses offered at their high school. At the end
of the year, they take a test to see if they score high
enough to get college credit. The cost of the test is
more than offset by the value of the college credit that
will be awarded to your student if he or she passes. It's
important to note that not all colleges accept these
credits, so it will be important to check with the admissions office of the college of your choice. A sec-
ondary benefit of these courses is that they can help
students get into college, because having AP and IB
credit makes for very good résumé fodder in college
applications. It shows ambition and a good work
ethic. For information regarding your state's programs, go to the National Association for College Admission Counseling Web site (www.nacacnet.org).

Start higher education at a community college first.
Community colleges can save you thousands of dollars. Students can attend two years and transfer to a
university to complete their education. Think of it as
a half-price sale for education: buy two years at full
price; get two for half off (or more). The average
community college tuition rate is 40 percent of the
average tuition at four-year public colleges and 10
percent of the average tuition at four-year private institutions. If your child attends a community college
for two years, you'll not only save money on tuition,
you'll also save on room and board and transportation by sticking close to home. The key to getting
the most value for your education dollar is to make

sure these college credits are transferable and to
assure they're working toward the four-year college
goal.

Did You Know?

*One of the coolest ways to pay for college is to let your
local school district help pay for it while your child is
still in high school. Many school districts now partner
with local colleges to offer college credit for high school
students who take classes at a nearby community college. Consequently, these classes count toward both the
high school and college degree requirements.*

*Be aware that these programs vary from district
to district and state to state. In some cases, the dual-
enrollment classes take place in the high school during
the regular school day. Other programs require students
to attend classes on the college campus, alongside other
college students. Some programs may charge nominal
tuition and others are subsidized by the school district.*

*For more information, go to www.hsc.org/chaos-high
school.html#college, www.powerstudents.com/high
school/hs_askexperts/1198h.shtml, www.houghton.k12
.mi.us/highschool/hsstudent-handbook.htm#Dual
Enrollment.*

NONTRADITIONAL OPTIONS

⌗ If you or your spouse have some latitude in your
   career, consider working at a local college for the

tuition benefits it would afford your child. Most universities offer some form of tuition remission to their full-time employees, and others extend the benefit to part-time employees as well.

- Check into military options. By going into the military as an enlisted person, students can serve their commitment and get significant money for college ($50,000 or more in many cases). By pursuing the ROTC route, your child will go to college first then enter the military as an officer. If your children go to a military academy, they pay only a nominal entrance fee (we paid $2,500 for our son Philip to enter the U.S. Naval Academy) and get an education valued at $400,000 with a guaranteed job at graduation. They have at least a five-year commitment to serve in the military after graduation. After three years in the job, they'll make at least $72,000 per year, and after fifteen years in the military, they'll make around $108,000 or much more in the civilian sector.[1]

- Check employer benefits. Many companies offer tuition reimbursement packages. A National Compensation Survey shows that 67 percent of employers offer financial assistance to employees seeking work-related college degrees.[2]

- Earn free money. Find organizations such as Upromise that reward you with money for college each time you buy products and services from participating companies. Membership is free at www.upromise.com, and you can receive money in a college savings account on nearly everything you buy, so be sure to

check this Web site before making any purchases.
Also find free contests to enter like Tuition Tales,
found at www.upromise.com that offer money
for higher education expenses. Sometimes www
.fastweb.com lists scholarships as well as contests.

⌗ Consider getting involved with an organization such
as Teach for America (www.teachforamerica.com),
the Peace Corps (www.peacecorps.gov), and Ameri-
corps (www.americorps.org). They offer educational
service awards to students seeking cash and a way to
make a difference in the world. The best part is that
unlike other scholarships and grants, these service
awards won't affect any federal financial aid eligibility. Even if your student has already acquired student
loans, organizations including the Army National
Guard, National Health Service Corps, and the National Institutes of Health all sponsor loan forgive-
ness programs that turn borrowed cash into free
dough in exchange for postgraduate service.

TRADITIONAL OPTIONS

⌗ Open a 529 plan. This is an education savings plan
operated by a state or educational institution designed to help families set aside funds for future
college costs. As long as the plan satisfies a few
basic requirements, the federal tax law provides
special tax benefits to the plan participant (see Section 529 of the Internal Revenue Service found at
www.irs.gov).

Various 529 plans are usually categorized as

Did You Know?

An Ivy League college education isn't necessarily all that it purports to be when you count the cost of attending that college versus the higher earning power that the Ivy League college is suppose to provide. In a recent study by SmartMoney *magazine, the payback ratio was calculated for the top public schools, Ivy League schools, and liberal arts schools. The study checked incomes for graduates three years and fifteen years after graduation. Texas A&M ranked number one with an average payback of 315 percent. Washington and Lee's payback was 140 percent and was the number-one liberal arts school. Princeton's average payback was 132 percent. This study supports the idea of buying as much school as you can afford without going into excessive student loan debt.*[3]

---

either prepaid or savings, although some have elements of both. Every state offers a 529 plan, and it's up to each state to decide what it will look like. Go to www.finaid.org to review your state plan. Parents can invest in any state's plan, no matter where they live and regardless of what plan they choose, and the beneficiary can attend any college or university in the country. What's more, grandparents and other benefactors can contribute money to a 529 plan. However, 529 plans may crimp a child's ability to receive financial aid in the future. It is important to review the state ratings for residents and nonresidents,

as some are rated better than others. These plans are
growing in popularity.

⊞ Check out prepaid tuition plans. Many states and
educational institutions allow parents to pay tomorrow's tuition expenses at today's prices. A 529 prepaid plan is offered by the individual states or
educational institutions and is prepaid similarly to a
529 plan but with less risk. Prepaid plans allow parents to pay tomorrow's expenses at today's prices, either by the year or by the credit hour. The
drawbacks are that even though parents can often
transfer some of these plans to other state colleges or
private tuitions, those schools do not guarantee the
same services and prices. Thus college students could
come up short. Contributions to prepaid plans
might also reduce a student's eligibility for financial
aid on a dollar-to-dollar basis, more than with a 529
plan. If the child does not attend college, the contributions are refundable, but there might be a cancel-
lation fee and/or loss of interest earned. It's
important to compare 529 plans to find the plan
that works best for your family. You can go to
www.savingforcollege.com to review the latest up-
dates to these various plans. In general, 529 plans are
best if parents (1) don't expect to qualify for financial
aid, (2) are conservative or novice investors, and (3)
understand the risks.

⊞ Apply for scholarships. Millions of scholarship dollars go unclaimed every year. For example, Sallie
Mae (www.salliemae.com) has more than 1.9 million scholarships totaling $16 billion. This is free

lunch money that parents or prospective students who are willing to do some detective work may find more quickly than they think. Similarly, www.fast web.com has more than 1.3 million scholarships to research. Don't forget to have students apply for local civic organizations' and community scholarships as well—high school counselors should have a list of these scholarships. This route is not for the faint of heart. I've talked to parents who said, "My child applied for twelve scholarships and never heard back from any of them." Trust me, you have to apply for a lot more than a dozen scholarships to see results in most cases.

Some of the students I interviewed made "applying for scholarships" their official part-time job during their junior and senior years. They applied for hundreds of scholarships, and each of them garnered $300,000+ in scholarship money for their efforts.

▩ Use Series EE U.S. Savings Bonds. If you use the income from these bonds to pay for education expenses, that interest may be excluded from taxes. But this exclusion is phased out beyond certain income levels.

▩ Check out zero-coupon bonds. The interest on these bonds is deferred until they mature, when it is paid in a lump sum. Parents do have to pay income tax on interest as it accrues each year the bond is held. It's often wise to "ladder" these bonds, where the bonds come to maturity during each year of the child's college career.

⌗ Consider Coverdell Education Savings Accounts (ESA). This will allow up to $2,000 of pretaxed income to be invested annually if the modified adjusted gross income is less than $95,000 as a single tax filer or $190,000 to $220,000 as a married couple filing jointly in the tax year in which the money is contributed. The $2,000 maximum contribution limit is gradually reduced if the modified adjusted gross income exceeds these limits. There are limits on how much can be invested based on income, and the funds must be spent before the child turns thirty. This education IRA will not interfere with the parents' ability to invest in a tax-deferred annuity in their own retirement account, but it will count heavily against the student when financial aid packages are calculated.

Because Coverdell IRA funds can be rolled into a 529 plan without penalty, parents can sidestep its principal drawbacks—the age limit and the fact that the IRA counts as the child's asset, which can adversely affect his or her ability to receive need-based loans. Therefore, a Coverdell account may be the best single investment option for parents whose income is below $50,000. The accounts are easier and less expensive to set up than 529 plans, and people in this lower tax bracket aren't usually able to take advantage of the maximum lifetime contributions allowed under a 529, which range from $110,000 to $305,000, because they don't pay that much tax in the first place.

⌗ Talk with the financial aid office. The university's financial aid office is a clearinghouse of information.

A good financial aid office will not only help students determine what loans they qualify for but will also steer them to participating lenders who are offering the best terms and service. Parents can do their own assessment by visiting www.college board.com's Paying for College Web page calculator found at www.payingforcollege.com.

🔲 Be sure to fill out the FAFSA (Free Application for Student Financial Aid) form. The FAFSA (found at www.fafsa.ed.gov) is the first step in applying for aid. It includes:

1. need-based guaranteed loans. (Stafford Loans are variable, while Perkins Loans are fixed.)
2. grants—Pell Grants and the Federal Supplemental Education Opportunity Grant each provide a gift up to a designated amount per student per student year.
3. work-study. Students can receive up to $2,000 per year, 25 percent of it matched by the participating institution, from the federal work-study program.

Some other options that the financial aid office might offer are tuition deals when your student is a freshman. Some schools may allow you to lock in your student's tuition for four years if you are willing to pay more the first year. By choosing that option, some families are saving a boatload of money by the time their student is in his or her junior and senior years because many universities raise tuition every year by as much as 8 percent. The only caveat is that if you leave the school, you don't get a refund on the premium you paid that first year. State loans and grants are also available, and the financial aid office should be able to quickly assess the student's eligibility.

⌖ Live at home. Room and board are oftentimes the most expensive part of college. By living with parents, grandparents, or other relatives, a student can pay as he goes in school because he doesn't have this major expense. We have no problem with one of our children living at home while earning his way through college.

⌖ Emancipate your child. In some cases, I've spoken with parents who can no longer afford out-of-state tuition for their child and/or the parents' income is just high enough that they do not qualify for any federal assistance. They took the rather drastic step of "cutting off" their child and declaring him or her emancipated, which makes the student responsible for all bills, taxes, etc. The parents no longer claim the child on their income tax and are no longer required to fill out paperwork as if they were part of the student's financial backup plan. The student can then establish state residency and get in-state tuition after a year, then he or she can also apply for federal grants and loans as well as financially based scholarships.

⌖ For more practical aspects of specific ways you can pay for college, e-mail assistant@elliekay.com and put "College Crunches" in the subject line. Our offices will send you a wonderful resource file to help you fund a quality education for a fraction of the debt. It could help make the difference between thirty years of student loan debt or a debt-free college experience!

Did You Know? —

Plenty of state schools offer reduced tuition for residents. The price difference between a state and private school is astounding. You will find that all expenses can be covered (including room and board) at a state school for the same price as tuition alone at a private school.

∽

Question:

My husband and I just had our first baby and everyone has been pressuring us about starting a college fund. Besides doing the obvious savings account, are there other options?

Answer:

Congratulations! Babies are wonderful. If you think the pressure is strong *now* to save money for college, try *not* doing anything and getting to your child's high school graduation without that money. *That's* pressure!

Parents of young children can start saving now for education in a tax-smart way by investing in the Uniform Gifts to Minors Act (UGMA). With an UGMA in the child's name, the government will tax that income at the child's marginal tax bracket rather than at the parents' tax rate. For example, if your beautiful bouncing three-year-old daughter has interest income of $700, the tax on that is zero. If she has income of $1,400, the next $700 is taxed at her 10 percent rate. If you're in the 28 percent bracket in 2009, the tax on the $1,400 total would be around

$400. Your daughter is only paying $70, so you've just saved $350 more for her college education.

The account must be registered in the child's name. An adult (usually a parent or grandparent) serves as custodian and is responsible for investing and managing the assets. But the child is the beneficial owner, meaning the assets really belong to the child.

At age eighteen (in most states), control of the assets must be turned over to the child (which could be a disadvantage for this plan when it comes to financial aid qualifications). All states offer UGMAs, and many have adopted the Uniform Transfers to Minors Act, or UTMA, as well. An UGMA allows children to own stocks, bonds, mutual funds, and other securities, along with real estate. Under UTMA, parents can delay giving the assets to the child until age twenty-one.

12

Save Big on
Everything Else!

12-Minute Tip #11: By going to my Web site's Tool
Center calculator (www.elliekay.com) for minimum
payments on credit cards, you'll see that if you pay
the 2 percent minimum payment for a credit card
debt of $10,000 at an interest rate of 18 percent, it
will cost you $28,900 in interest and take fifty-seven
years to pay off. But if you improve your FICO
(Fair Isaac Corporation) credit score just a little bit
and lower the annual percentage rate (APR) to 9
percent and then pay 3 percent of the minimum, it
will take only four years to pay off and save you
$6,240 per year in interest! Take twelve minutes to
set up a new minimum payment plan and save
$1,200 or more each year, depending on your total
credit card debt.

When I was growing up, one of our neighbors, Mrs. Kooperman, had a poodle named FiFi. On hot Texas afternoons,
Mrs. Kooperman would sunbathe, with Fifi lying close by
in the shade. The odd thing about Mrs. Kooperman was
that she freckled and didn't tan, and the odd thing about

FiFi was that, after she was groomed, she would get sun-burned if she emerged from her shade. They made a fascinating pair to observe for a seven-year-old neighbor girl such as myself!

Credit card companies also own a dog. This one is named FeeFee, and their little poodle knows a lot of tricks. FeeFee will burn you with late fees, overlimit fees, cash advance fees, and shorter grace periods. And that's not even counting the interest you're paying on the money you spend on credit!

Entire books are written on credit debt, and I spend several chapters in *Living Rich for Less* going deeper on the topic. But for the next several pages we're going to focus on how you can save money, pay down your debt, and work to get a better credit rating.

෴

CREDIT SAVINGS

- ⌗ When your credit card bill arrives, pay the minimum payment right away—especially if you have a twenty-one-day billing cycle. You can always send a larger payment at the end of the month—and hopefully you will, because it's important to start paying down your debt as soon as possible. That will save you money on interest accruals.
- ⌗ Pay the original minimum that you started with on each credit card. If you continue to pay the amount of the *original* minimum payment, you will soon find that the *required* minimum is reduced. If your payment remains at the higher amount, then you are

paying on the principal and saving on interest by paying the debt off early. So when your original minimum is $100, and six months later it is only $90, you continue to pay at least the $100. Thus you're easily paying more than the minimum—plus, it is already a part of your monthly spending plan so you don't feel the pinch that sometimes accompanies paying more than the minimum.

- Automate your payments. Whether you normally carry a balance or not, you can set up an automated payment with your banking institution by going to your credit card's online site. The payment would be for a few dollars more than your estimated minimum payment each month. This way you can make sure you won't have a late fee. Most consumers get six late fees per year on a variety of bills at an average penalty of $30 each. Save $180 per year.

- Ask! If you are charged a late fee and do not have a history of late charges or other delinquencies, call the lender and ask them to remove the late fee. They may do this if you take the time to ask—especially if you fit the "good customer" criteria.

- If you need cash, use your debit card instead of your credit card. If you get into the habit of getting cash on your credit card, you not only pay exorbitant additional fees, but you could go into greater debt and have little or nothing to show for it. Avoid a $100 cash advance three times a year: save an average of $45 per year.

- About two and a half months before your card is set to renew, or if you receive a notice that your lender is replacing your old card with a new and improved version, call the credit card company and ask what the annual fee will be. If you are a good customer and have a solid history with this company, ask them to waive the annual fee in order to keep you as a happy customer. Ask two of your credit card companies if you can avoid paying the annual fee for being a good customer: save $40 per card, or $80. Or better yet...

⌘ Make sure the credit cards you have charge a low rate (not just a temporary introductory rate) that is fixed (not subject to increase) and with no annual fee. If you have a temporary rate, try to get it converted to a fixed rate.

⌘ Pay attention to the notices you get in the mail. Your creditor is required to notify you of all changes in advance. This includes any adjustment in grace periods, interest rates, and card provider changes. In the fine-print brochure you receive, you are allowed to decline the new terms and pay off your account under the old terms, but you would also have to give up the card and not charge new items.

In tough economies, credit card companies are fond of raising interest rates. You may have had an introductory rate or a relatively low rate and then receive notification that the interest rate is going up. Be sure you read the details, because in some cases the interest rate on the debt you've accrued can remain at the lower rate, but the first time you use the card after the notification, it could possibly be taken as an "acceptance" of the new rate for that card. Call the credit card company and be sure you understand the details. You might want to stop using that card in order to keep the rates low, and if you have to charge, use another card whose rates are lower.

⊞ Don't fall for those "save 10 percent today on everything in the store if you open a charge account with us" pitches at the checkout. Lenders consistently review credit reports. If you are opening too many charge accounts (even a 0 percent APR for furniture), your credit rating could take a hit with an increased APR on your credit card. So that 10 percent you save could cost you a whole lot more!

⊞ Be sure not to charge more than 50 percent of the available credit on any credit card. Getting it down to 30 percent is even better. For example, if you have a card with a limit of $8,000, in order to keep the best rates, you should carry no more than $4,000 as a revolving balance on that card.

⊞ If you are maxing out your credit limit, it could send a message to lenders that you are getting into debt overload with the potential of not having the means to pay your bills. Consequently, you could get hit with a higher rate because you are a greater risk to the lender. Mind your limits on credit and checking accounts, unlike the average consumer who exceeds her limits twice a year. Save $56.

⊞ Pay even $5 more than the minimum due. In the past, lenders seemed to encourage borrowers to carry a balance and only pay the minimum payment due on the debt. They even reinforced this concept by making the minimum payment only 1 percent of the total debt instead of the standard 2 to 3 percent. But things have changed in recent years. Those minimum-paying customers are now viewed as potential risks. Can they pay all their debts? Are they paying the minimums because they are living month to month with no additional funds yet still have available credit? Not only does minimum-paying mean accruing tons of interest, it could indicate that you are an at-risk customer who may be more likely to default on a loan. Some minimum-paying customers are now having their rates raised to as much as 28 percent or more simply because they don't attempt to pay down the balance.

⚎ Knowledge is power. Check your credit report at least three times a year. You can do it for free by going to www.annualcreditreport.com and even get a copy of your report. Each of the three major credit-reporting agencies is required by law to give you a free copy once a year. You can order these at the aforementioned site for free—stagger your requests to one every four months and you'll have a good pulse on possible fraud and any errors that might arise. Order each of your three credit reports for free instead of paying for them: save $60 per year.

Dispute errors, check for fraud (possible identity theft), and close department store cards you don't use. Or contact any of the three credit reporting agencies directly at:

- Equifax: 1-800-685-1111 or www.equifax com.
- Experian (formerly TRW): 1-888-397-3742 or www.experian.com.
- TransUnion: 1-800-888-4213 or www.trans union.com.

▓ Your credit rating, or FICO score, affects your rate.
If you don't know your credit rating, you can be sure
your lender does! Basically, your credit score is the
number that is calculated from data in your credit
report. These scores help lenders make fair credit
decisions since FICO scores reveal facts to them that
relate to your general risk. The factors involved in
the rating are based purely on the numbers and not
on race, religion, nationality, gender, or marital status. While some people assume that these last two
factors (gender and marital status) are credit risk factors, that is a misconception.

Customers with a lower credit rating (generally
600 or less depending upon the lender) will pay a
higher APR. I talk more about FICO scores in my
book *Living Rich for Less*—what they are, why
they're important, and what you can do to improve
them.

Although some women may not have credit
scores as high as their male counterparts, it usually
has more to do with whether they have an estab-
lished credit history of their own and developed a
good individual credit history rather than from joint
accounts. Many women do not realize that their
individual FICO score is a different number from
their husband's. Each has his or her own rating.
In the case of joint credit, the factors involved will
affect both spouses, but the individual numbers are
still separate.

To see what your FICO score is, go to www
.myfico.com or www.creditexpert.com to find out!

🎴 If you want to transfer your balance to another credit card, before you commit, read the fine print to avoid a 3 percent balance transfer fee on total transfer amounts of $3,000. Save $90.

🎴 Cut up all but one or two credit cards and cancel all other open credit accounts. This will help minimize the temptation to impulse buy as well as serve to keep you within your goal of no new debt. But before you cut up those cards, make sure you close the newest credit lines first as the older the credit line, the better your FICO score. So cancel the credit card you've had for a year rather than the one you've had for eight years.

🎴 Don't be deceived by some of the reward cards—do the math on those cards. For example, most cards that offer frequent-flier miles require that you earn 25,000 miles (at one mile per dollar = $25,000 spent) in order to buy *one* ticket (which averages $250 to $300). That means you are earning one cent for every dollar you spend. On the other hand, some reward cards can be very rewarding, and I try to take advantage of "double-dipping" by signing up for hotel, airline, restaurants, etc., who are partners with my reward card. I regularly earn free flights for a third of the usual reward charges needed.

Just be careful that these reward cards don't subliminally encourage you to overspend on your credit card, and you'll have a good balance.

For a list of credit cards by category (low-rate, no annual fee, etc.) go to www.bankrate.com or www.cardtrak.com. Other tools that are available to

help you get the card that is right for you are
www.getsmart.com or www.creditcardgoodies.com.

🔢 Make it your policy never to use credit cards for impulse purchases. As a matter of fact, it's best to leave
your credit cards at home. Don't even carry them to
the mall or to the store.

Did You Know?

*I don't want you to get panicky over the idea that Big
Brother is watching you, but…Big Brother is watching you. Lenders track your charges, payments, and
spending habits. Part of this is good, because if you
suddenly start charging lingerie in France and swimsuits in Germany and you've never charged anything
outside your state before, this Big Brother practice can
alert the credit card issuer to possible fraud.*

*Like so many things that can be good but may
have a negative underbelly, you need to be aware of
your own habits because they could work against you
and make you a prime marketing target for additional
credit card offers and products that may not be in your
best interest to pursue. This awareness can save you
money on interest and fees.*

INVESTMENTS: 401(K)S AND IRAS

🔢 Prevent an unqualified removal of $10,000 from
a 401(k) or IRA, which will cost you in penalties,
interest, and tax. Save $1,050.

🔀 Take tax benefits that can move you into a lower income tax bracket after retirement (the 15 percent
bracket as opposed to the 30 percent bracket). Save
$150 per $1,000 contributed. For example, if you
contributed only $2,000 per year for twenty years:
save $6,000 when you withdraw the money after
retirement.

🔀 Invest a 401(k) in mutual funds and claim the matching benefit that many companies offer. We did this at
100 percent up to $5,000. Earn $5,000 per year.

The matching portion of this fund from your
employer may not be as high as 100 percent, but it's
still important to contribute to your 401(k). Even
employers who are cutting back to a mere 25 percent match are still an excellent deal for workers. If
your 401(k) fund doesn't perform well in a bad
economy, you still have the 25 percent return of the
employer's match. So don't let dwindling balances in
your fund keep you from investing—especially when
your employer is matching those funds! If your fund
performs badly, the fallout will eat into the employer's matching portion long before it touches the
principle of the amount you have contributed. Plus,
the other obvious benefit is that in the 401(k) plan,
your investment earnings (interest, dividends, and
capital gains) within the plan accumulate tax free
until they are withdrawn.

🔀 Keep contributing! If you don't you will miss the tax
deferral, which is a humongous benefit. If you're in
the 28 percent tax bracket and put $10,000 in your
tax-favored plan (either an IRA or your 401[k]), it
costs you only $7,300 of actual take-home money.

This means that the tax deferral alone is an instant 28 percent return on your money.

⌘ Set up your contributions as an automatic withdrawal from your paycheck, and you'll never miss what you never see. Remember that pretax contributions are the fastest route to building the kind of wealth you will need for retirement.

⌘ There are two basic IRA options that you should evaluate and choose between in order to continue to grow wealth through investments: the traditional IRA and the Roth IRA. Choose a Roth IRA if you can do without the tax break right now (or if you don't qualify for a tax-deductible IRA). It's a more flexible instrument because:

- It allows you to withdraw your contributions at any time, penalty- and tax-free.
- You do not have to take mandatory distributions at age seventy and a half.

Choose a traditional IRA if you need the tax deduction right now, if you have not contributed to a 401(k), or if you anticipate paying taxes at a significantly lower rate in retirement.

⌘ Fund your IRA at least once a year. Everyone has until April 15 to make a contribution to an IRA for the previous year—it's not like you have to make it by December 31. This is good because it gives you time to gather the money to put into your IRA. I recommend that you figure out how much you'll contribute for the year (let's say $2,000 for you and $2,000 for your spouse), divide it by 52 weeks ($38.46 per person), and allocate that amount as an automatic withdrawal to go to the account you've set aside for funding your IRA. When it's automatic and made before you get your paycheck, it's a lot easier to prioritize it. The goal is to work toward fully funding IRAs for both you and your spouse (a weekly allotment of $76.92). When tax day rolls around, you'll fund your IRA and start saving for next year's fund.

Did You Know?

I have loads more tips on investment smarts. If you're interested in learning more, I've got a deal for you. Just e-mail LivingRich@elliekay.com, and in the subject line enter "Investment Ally." We will send you a special link for this resource. This is available only to Living Rich for Less *and* The Little Book of Big Savings *readers, and this section of the Web site is not viewable without the specific link. In our Investment Ally, you'll find greater detail on some of the investment sections referenced in this chapter.*

Question:

I've tried not to use my credit card, but I'm never sure how much money I have on hand, so I just charge things. Is there an easy way to limit my spending?

Answer:

You bet there is! One of the biggest problem areas that can throw off your spending plan in a matter of seconds—

sending it reeling toward disaster—is the use of credit. If overspending is an issue, you may want to look at making your policy one of cash only. Some people set up an envelope system for cash. Every two weeks they place an allotted amount of cash in envelopes marked "food," "entertainment," "gas," etc. When the money runs out— you're done, until the end of the two-week period. A regular peek at the amount of cash left in each envelope is a vivid reminder of your commitments.

Question:

I don't believe all the hype everyone says about credit card spending. Yes, I use my card, and although I don't pay off the entire amount, I pay on time every month and simply consider it just another bill, like my mortgage or electric bills. What's the big deal?

Answer:

Well, at least you're being honest! I hear this same attitude from a lot of people. It doesn't matter if their cards are maxed out, they figure if they keep paying, they're fine.

But it's shocking to me that the average consumer debt in the United States is steadily on the rise (even in our current economy) and currently stands at $8,500 per person.[1] This doesn't include debt for a mortgage or car loans, only consumer and credit card debt. Look at this chart to see for yourself how much you're really paying and *overpaying* by staying in debt. If you overspend your income by only $100 per month, in ten years you will be more than $30,000 in debt:

Based on charging $100 to credit cards each month

Year	Amount Over Budget	Accumulated Interest	End-of-Year Debt
1	$1,200	$104	$1,304
2	1,200	463	2,863
3	1,200	1,128	4,728
4	1,200	2,157	6,957
5	1,200	3,621	9,621
6	1,200	5,608	16,617
8	1,200	11,572	21,172
9	1,200	15,818	26,618
10	1,200	21,129	33,129
11	1,200	27,714	40,914
12	1,200	35,821	50,221
13	1,200	45,749	61,349
14	1,200	57,855	74,655
15	1,200	72,562	90,562
Totals	$18,000	$72,562	$90,562

This chart illustrates vividly how a modest amount of accumulating debt can cause a family's finances to self-destruct. It's basically the miracle of compounding interest either working for you or against you.

But let's take it one step further. It takes just one missed payment to mess up your credit score, which messes up just about everything else in your financial situation—such as applying for a mortgage, car loan, even insurance. Still think your debt isn't a big deal?

Question:

Help! I want to raise my credit score. What can I do?

Answer:

If only everyone felt that way. Sigh.

FICO scores are very important—they count for or against you when you apply for loans, mortgages, insurance, even rent. So you want your score to be high.

Try these three steps to improve your FICO score immediately:

1. Pay a day early rather than a day late (set up an automatic pay plan online).
2. Pay more than your minimum balance on each credit card (even $5 or $10 more).
3. Pay proportionally. Make sure your proportionality is not more than 50 percent on each card (if your card has a $6,000 limit, make sure you don't have more than $3,000 charged on it).

There you have it. Take up the challenge, and you'll be the winner in the end with an improved FICO and a better chance to recession-proof your credit score.

Question:

A friend of mine saves all her change. Does that really work?

Answer:

It does. But some people don't like messing with all that change. Another option for easy savings and investing is to commit to saving a dollar a day. If you invest one dollar a day for ten years at 10 percent interest you can earn $6,145.

Look at the following chart that shows what investing a dollar a day will yield. You could give up your daily candy bar and soda to help *more* than your waistline. Higher interest rates tend to be more speculative, so beware of the risks involved. You'll see it's worth the effort to save your dollar a day.

One Dollar a Day
Cumulative Return

Yrs.	Total Invested	5%	10%	15%	20%
10	$3,600	$4,658	$6,145	$8,257	$11,283
20	7,200	12,331	22,781	44,917	93,290
30	10,800	24,968	67,815	207,698	689,335
40	14,400	45,781	189,722	930,482	5,021,546
50	18,000	80,060	519,732	4,139,793	36,509,163

Question:

I'd like to start investing and I've heard good things about IRAs. How do I set one up?

Answer:

It's easy to set up an IRA.

Step 1: Find a discount broker. If you don't already have one, I suggest you look into opening a discount brokerage account. For a complete chart that compares different brokerage firms and the fees associated with them, go to Investment Ally (which I mentioned earlier in this chapter). This broker should be able to handle IRAs, Roth IRAs, rollover accounts, spouse IRAs, and education IRAs.

Step 2: Open and fund your account. Once you've

compared discount brokers and decided which one is the best fit for your financial needs, it's time to open your account. Most brokers have an online application you can complete and electronically transfer funds from your checking or savings account. However, some brokers require that you print out the form and mail it in with a check.

Step 3: Invest it! Once your check or electronic transfer has cleared, you're ready to start investing. That means deciding which stocks or mutual funds you want to buy or consulting your brokers for their opinion and instructing them to buy the stocks or mutual funds, thereby funding the account.

13

Save Big by Sharing

12-Minute Tip #12: By filing taxes jointly, a couple that makes $65,000 in the 25 percent tax bracket can give away their tithe of $6,500 and itemize their giving, and in the process gain a benefit of $1,625 in estimated tax savings. In order for you to be able to itemize and get your full donation deduction, take twelve minutes to get the proper documentation for each of your gifts. Not only will this save you worry in the event of an IRS audit, it will also allow you to take that deduction and, depending on your tax bracket and donation, could save you $1,200 or more on your taxes.

When our son Daniel was nine, he came up with the idea of keeping canned goods in our Suburban to hand out to people in need. We would give each person two cans of chili or pasta meals. When we first started doing this, the kids were so enthusiastic to help that they saw a homeless person behind every bush. One day we were driving down the road when then seven-year-old Philip yelled, "Hey! There's a homeless man!" He pointed toward a man on a bicycle.

"Philip!" I said, "That man is not homeless. His jeans are just dirty."

Philip sighed. "Well, he looked kind of lost to me. Maybe we could give him some clothes soap!"

It's the thought that counts.

The one principle that sets apart my approach to finances is the idea of saving for a reason beyond just your own well-being. I've always encouraged people to save in order to share—and it works. Some call it the law of reciprocity, some may call it the tithe, some call it being neighborly, and some call it giving back to your community. Whatever you call it, you will find that what you give comes back to you in a wide variety of ways.

If you truly look at what you have, it's a lot more than what so many people in our world have. And what a great feeling to know that even the smallest things you share can make a huge difference in the lives of people who are less fortunate. The rewards you receive in return are truly priceless: that feeling of helping someone else; the joy that comes in thinking about how much better that person or family's life can be simply because you said "yes" to sharing what you've been able to save.

In *Living Rich for Less,* I focus on the 10/10/80 Rule, which says that in order to live the fullest life, you should share your first 10 percent (called a tithe), save 10 percent, and spend 80 percent of your monthly income.

In the early years of our marriage when Bob and I had $40,000 in debt and couldn't make ends meet, we were tempted to ignore the sharing part of the 10/10/80 Rule and not give. But we truly believed in the spiritual aspect of giving: by sharing that first 10 percent, we would always be taken care of financially. It doesn't always add up quantitatively, but that doesn't mean it is exclusively anecdotal.

In other words, you can't always measure spiritual truth on the bottom line of a spreadsheet. You have to allow for the faith factor, which may not show up on the front end of a chart or graph or formula. But in our experience, it always showed up on the bottom line.

If we hoarded, we died financially, but when we opened up that channel of giving, we found new life. Sometimes it showed up in the most amazing ways, like when I won the main prize on a game show (*The Price Is Right*—that's a whole story on its own!) and we sold it for cash. Other times it was manifested in a humbling way—like when people gave us clothing that exactly fit our children and was a perfect provision.

With the thousands of dollars you can save by following the tips in the previous chapters, you can find lots of extra money to be able to share! Let's look at some ways you can share and some of the tangible rewards you can get from it.

༄

The Big Give

- With any buy-one-get-one-free deal (especially canned and boxed goods)—or when you combine coupons and store sales to get an item for pennies or for *free*—consider sharing these goods with a local food pantry or a family in need.
- The largest expenditure for Thanksgiving tends to be the meat. If you watch the sales, frequent buyer deals, and store coupons, you can get an amazing

deal on your big bird. Several Thanksgivings ago, Albertson's had a buy-one-get-one-free offer on their store-brand turkeys. Their competitor, IGA, had a special for a store-brand 12- to 15- pound turkey for $6 with a store coupon. Since Albertson's honors competitor's coupons, I was able to take the IGA coupon there and get the first turkey I bought for only $6. Since the buy one, get one free was a store special and not a coupon special, I got the second turkey for free. So I wound up with two fifteen-pound turkeys for only $6. I kept one and gave one to the Salvation Army, who was having a shortage on turkeys that year.

- If you're involved in a local church, donate your funds there. Your church helps teach your family spiritual values, runs kids' programs in the summers, provides food and clothing to orphanages, and sends money to victims of natural disasters. If you aren't part of a local church, you and your family are missing out on some incredible opportunities to have your unique spiritual needs met. Once you find your fit, partner with them financially to reach your community.

- Place all your expired coupons in a bag marked "Expired Coupons" and send them to a military family overseas who can use them in a military commissary up to six months past the expiration date. For an up-to-date list of bases to send your coupons, e-mail our offices at assistant@elliekay.com and put "Expired Coupons" in the subject line.

- Simplify! One of the best ways to help yourself and others at the same time is to tackle a room, closet, or even a piece of furniture and clean it out. In other words, get more organized. I recommend investing in a good organization book such as Marcia Ramsland's *Simplify Your Space: Create Order and Reduce Stress* found at www.organizingpro.com. For example, you could choose to start in a bedroom and go through the dresser drawers. Take everything out of each drawer, and put it in one of three piles: (1) Give Away, (2) Throw Away, and (3) Keep. The "give away" pile obviously gets donated. And your house feels less cluttered. A double bonus!

⌘ Call a nonprofit organization that needs and wants your donations. Some will even come and pick up your donations. In the process, you'll be helping to meet the needs of someone else in your community. Be sure to ask for an itemized receipt and keep track of the original value and the donated value of the items for tax purposes. Go to www.salvationarmyusa.org for an evaluation guide. If you do this with each room in your home (including the garage), not only will you address the clutter, you'll relieve stress in the process while helping others. Does it get any better than that?

⌘ Pay attention to information in your community about specific needs. This might be on fliers, in the newspaper, posted on a bulletin board, or in an interoffice memo. Don't ignore these needs. Instead, dedicate fifteen minutes toward collecting those specific items. If you gather only a few things, it will still help. It might be a matter of collecting your soda cans, gathering food items, or looking for specific items of clothing. You might even want to add some of these things to your shopping list and pick them up. If you begin to develop the mind-set of giving, the next time you hear of a need, you won't be inclined to think, *Oh no! Not again,* but rather, *I wonder how I can meet this need?* You don't have to be extravagant; it really is true that every little bit helps. Just give what you can and start where you are.

- Give the gift of life to a third-world child. Most sponsorships run anywhere from $25 to $35 per month and provide food, clothing, housing, and education. We've had the thrill of watching kids grow up under our sponsorship and go on to become leaders in their communities. Our family currently sponsors children from three reputable organizations:

  - **World Vision.** On their "Ways to Give" link, you can choose where you want your dollars to go. World Vision helps children in the United States as well as around the world. Go to www.worldvision.org or call 1-888-511-6598.

  - **Compassion International.** This organization is tuned in to crisis and special needs as well as the general monthly needs of children around the world. It encourages communication with your child, and you have the chance to see photos and receive news of how he or she is doing in school. It's a great project for your family. Go to www.compassion.com.

- **Mission of Joy.** This is a lesser-known organization that was started by two air force captains when they saw the needs in India. Twenty years later, thousands of people have been positively affected by this nonprofit organization. Almost 97 percent of the monthly contributions go directly to India because the ministry uses volunteer help and has little overhead. Go to www.missionofjoy.org.

Did You Know?

When asked why people don't sponsor a child or give to a national or global charity, most will say they aren't certain that their money really goes to that child or that program. Some of the greatest concerns are legitimate: the idea that donations go to fund-raising efforts, to overhead, or to large executive salaries. The answer for this concern is simple: go to the Better Business Bureau Wise Giving Alliance at www.give.org or call 1-703-276-0100 to get a copy of the BBB Wise Giving Guide. This will help you decide which organization to choose. The BBB Wise Giving Alliance offers guidance to donors on making informed giving decisions through their charity evaluations, various tips publications, and the quarterly Wise Giving Guide.

REWARDS

▦ Get a tax deduction for sharing. When you donate groceries to a nonprofit organization (or a church), ask for a receipt. Keep your grocery receipts and highlight the donated item. Current tax laws allow you to deduct the value of the item as a donation (the price *before* coupons since coupons are considered *cash tendered*). If you donate to an organization, be sure to drop off your donations during business hours so you can secure a tax-deductible receipt. You'll need to itemize, and I recommend you check with a tax specialist each year to keep up-to-date on this deduction.

⌘ Save those receipts! If you itemize on your taxes, it is critical that you get tax-deductible receipts for all donations to any nonprofit organization, including Goodwill, The Salvation Army, Vietnam Veterans of America, Military Order of the Purple Heart, and homeless shelters. You should save *all* receipts for donations of $250 or more. So if you give away more than $250 worth of clothing throughout the year, you should have saved all the receipts that will add up to that amount. You must donate these to a nonprofit organization or have that organization donate it to a needy individual. The money you donate directly to a needy person is *not* deductible. It would be better to donate the amount to your church and have the church anonymously send the clothing donation to the family in need. One family I know donated a total of $800 in items to Goodwill and saved about $224 on their taxes.

⌘ Double up. We've already mentioned that you should get a tax-deductible receipt for your giving, but what if you're just getting started and don't think you'll have enough deductions to itemize on your income tax return? You could "double up" on your giving by deferring your normal year-end gifts that would be given in December until January of the new year. Then give your regular gifts at the end of that new year too. This doubling up will likely give you the amount you need to itemize.

❊ Start your own foundation. When the stock market eventually comes back, if you've bought stock while it's low and if you are fortunate enough to have a large gain from that stock or mutual fund that you have held for more than a year, consider using it to become what is essentially your own foundation. For example, if you own $5,000 worth of stock that you bought years ago for only $1,000, you can donate the stock by setting up a Fidelity Charitable Gift Fund account (call 1-800-682-4438, or go to www.charitablegift.org). By doing this, you get an immediate $5,000 tax deduction and save having to pay taxes on the $4,000 gain. In the years to come, as that $5,000 grows, you can instruct the company that manages your foundation on where to donate the proceeds. Besides Fidelity, charitable gift funds are also available through Vanguard (1-888-383-4483 or www.vanguardcharitable.org) and Schwab (1-800-746-6216 or www.schwabcharitable.org).

Sometimes setting up this kind of foundation in addition to your other cash and household item donations can lower your overall taxable income to the point where you are in a lower tax bracket—thereby saving even more on your taxes.

❊ Train your children. You may want to allow your children to manage a donation of a predetermined amount ($25, $50, $100, or whatever you have budgeted). Around November, let your kids know that you will allow them to manage a donation. They get to research a variety of nonprofit organizations and decide which one will receive their donation. Then donate the amount in your child's name. You get the tax benefit, your child gets the thank-you note, and you both feel good about giving.

Did You Know?

Tax savings is one of my favorite ways to save! But they're also the wild card. Taxes are based on a number of detailed factors that change from year to year and person to person. Always make sure you check with your tax professional before making any financial decisions that will impact your overall tax liability.

❧

Question:

Lots of people give to the local church, food pantry, or homeless shelter. But are there other places I can share my donations?

Answer:

You bet! Check out these other options:

- Crisis pregnancy centers. These centers provide assistance to women in crisis pregnancies by giving tangible help in the form of medical care, clothes, toiletries, baby food, groceries, and sometimes housing.

- Orphanages and children's homes. There may not be a local orphanage, but your church or civic organization may have regular access to these institutions. Contact these organizations and see what kind of needs list they may have. Often these lists are specific due to the age, gender, and size of their children as well as their nutritional requirements.

- Women's shelters. Women and children who seek these shelters often arrive with only the clothes on their backs. These shelters especially need trial-size toiletries, as their occupants may stay for a day or for several months, as well as children's and women's clothing. Look in the Yellow Pages under "Spouse Abuse" for the phone number. Don't be surprised if you are asked to drop off these donations at a downtown office rather than the home itself—confidentiality is necessary for the protection of these clients.

- Over a six-month period, I acquired thirty-five bottles of hair coloring free with my couponing. These were donated to this shelter with the understanding that the women could exchange them at the local grocery store for the right shade. Sometimes it's the little things that make the difference in a difficult situation.

- Postal workers food drive. Every year postal workers collect millions of pounds of non-perishable food for people in need. In addition, there are Boy Scout and Girl Scout food drives and others throughout the community. Your child's school or your church may also have occasional food drives to stock community food pantries. Brenda Conway contacted me to say, "I used to donate two cans of food to my son's Boy Scout food drive—now I'm able to donate two bags of groceries, and I don't spend any more than I did before."

Question:

I've always donated to the local pantry, but I've never asked for receipts before. How much can you really save on your taxes through donations?

Answer:

The 12-Minute Tip at the beginning of this chapter shows you one amount. Take a look at some of these other amounts, depending on your marital and tax-filing status.

A single person donating $1,500 in December and another $3,950 throughout the next year (in cash and other donations) would either reach the minimum to itemize or, if in the 15 percent bracket, would then save approximately $900 in taxes.

A married couple filing jointly in the 33 percent tax bracket could donate $8,000 in tithe and another $3,000 in nonprofit household-item donations to save a total of $3,597 in taxes.

Your kids' donations would count toward the overall donations as well. In an itemized package, a family in the

25 percent bracket with three children donating $100 each would see an approximate tax benefit of $75.

It's important to remember that these amounts are *not* set in stone, though. Tax options change all the time. So although you can bet you'll definitely save money by donating and getting receipts, the amounts you'll save may vary. So, as always, check with your tax professional for up-to-date, up-to-the-minute information.

Question:

I love the idea of sharing. But my problem is that I'll start something and then forget to follow through. Any tips?

Answer:

I could write an entire book on that!

One of the easiest ways I've found to keep track of your giving is to write down three areas where you would like to start giving your money, assets, time, or talents. Write the date by which you plan to start your giving and leave a space for when you've achieved this goal.

14

Now *This* Is What
I Call Living!

Baker's Dozen Tip: Hey, I'm allowed to donate an extra big tip to you! By establishing a spending plan and sticking to it, our large family on one income was able to dig out of $40,000 in debt in only two and a half years. With me as a SAHM (stay-at-home mom) during the following fifteen years, living on a budget allowed us to take nice vacations, furnish our home tastefully, clothe the kids in style, pay cash for eleven cars, give away three of those cars, buy two five-bedroom homes (one after selling the other), and support more than thirty nonprofit organizations in a dozen different countries by giving away more than $100,000. All because we stuck to a spending plan.

Okay, I have a confession to make. I've been holding out on you. Well, not really *holding out,* per se. But I *have* been keeping something from you. (Is that the same thing?) I've been keeping a secret. A special secret that leads to the biggest savings of all.

Want to know what it is? I'll give you a hint. It starts

with the letter *b,* and if you've been following the tips in the previous chapters, you're already on your way to making it really work for you.

Can't figure it out? Want another hint? Okay, the first part of the word rhymes with one of my favorite foods—*fudge.*

Yep, you guessed it! *Budget.* And that's what you've been working on through this whole book! Pat yourself on the back. Well done!

I specifically avoided using the dreaded *budget* word throughout this book because that word carries with it a lot of eye rolls, heavy sighs, and gritted teeth. People are tired of hearing the word, using the word, even *thinking* about the word. But the truth is that if you truly want to save big, you have to know where your money is going. The best and easiest way to do that? You guessed it right again. You need to be proactive about setting up a budget that you can follow and track where your money is going.

Studies show over and over that people who follow a clear-cut budget actually save more money, make smarter financial decisions, and live happier lives. People who just "go with the flow," on the other hand, really do go with the flow—they spend themselves right down the river to the poor house.

Fortunately, I know you're not one of those "go with the flow" people anymore. Just by picking up this book and its companion *Living Rich for Less,* you're on your way to making healthy, happy, smart money choices.

Let's look briefly at putting together a 10/10/80 budget, which I discussed briefly in the previous chapter.

STEP 1: CALCULATE YOUR INCOME

The first step is to determine your monthly funds *after* state and federal income taxes and Social Security. Income includes salary, rents, notes, interest, dividends, tips, child support, and other forms of income. Enter the total on the line "net income" on the budget form included in the back of this book (page 198).

STEP 2: CALCULATE CURRENT SPENDING LEVELS

The next step is to calculate your *current* spending patterns. Be honest with everything. Fill in your current spending levels in the chart and be prepared for a reality check!

If you prefer online tools, then after you've worked through the 10/10/80 budget chart at the end of this book (page 198) and decided on a workable giving/saving/spending plan, you can go to www.elliekay.com to find a tool that will help meet your techie needs.

STEP 3: CALCULATE YOUR CURRENT SITUATION

Now take your net income and subtract your current spending to establish your overall spending (if you are married with or without kids, this would include the entire family spending). Are you spending more (through credit) than you make each month? Are you spending everything you make (with nothing going into savings)? Are there unexplained gaps in your current spending levels? Did you know that you (or your spouse) were hitting the ATM machine that many times each month or getting that much cash back on your debit card purchases? Are you saving as much as you need to? Or are you on target and healthy in your current giving, saving, and spending patterns? You'll find out the true picture by completing this section.

STEP 4: DETERMINE YOUR 10/10/80 BUDGET BASED ON LINE ITEMS

As you prepare to fill in your budget form, it's important to know what kinds of expenses to include in each category and to list any items your family has that are unique to your situation. Here is a basic list of line items that you should include in each category.

- Tithe/Charitable Donations: 10 percent to church, civic, or community donations.
- Savings: 10 percent to savings accounts, 401(k) funding, Roth IRA, or other IRA investments, regular savings for upcoming bills (insurance, taxes, etc.), and unexpected emergencies.
- Clothing/Dry Cleaning: 5 percent to new clothing and shoes, thrift store bargains, garage sale finds, dry cleaning, alterations, repairs, patterns, and sewing supplies.
- Education/Miscellaneous: 5 percent to tuition, books, music or other lessons, school supplies, newspapers, and miscellaneous expenses. The miscellaneous portion includes all other unbudgeted items and any debt payments.
- Food: 10 percent to groceries and meals eaten outside the home.

- Housing: 30 percent to mortgage or rent, property taxes, utilities (including phone, gas, water, and electricity), cleaning supplies, labor costs/maid, lawn care, pool care, tools and repair, household repairs, furniture and bedding, appliances, and garden equipment.
- Insurance: 5 percent includes life, home, and health insurance.
- Medical/Dental: 4 percent to doctor, dentist, eyeglasses, medicines, and vitamins.
- Recreation/Vacation/Gifts: 6 percent to entertainment, movies, hobbies, pets, television, sporting goods, toys, gifts, and vacations.
- Transportation: 15 percent to airline tickets, bus and taxi fares, car payments and insurance, car repairs and licenses, gasoline, and oil.

Budgeting is a kind of an adventure. There are boundaries, rules, and guidelines that work if you follow them carefully. But don't get discouraged if your current spending patterns are not where they will be one day as you continue to use the tips in this book and work toward your goal to follow the 10/10/80 budget.

Friendly Reminders!

Some things to keep in mind as you develop your financial plan:

1. **Set goals.** Begin with the end in mind. If you don't know where your family finances are going, how can you reach your desired destination? Goals are a road map to where you want to be.

2. **Be honest**. When you calculate current spending levels to determine your current budget, be sure to write down everything you spend over a three-month period. If you spend cash, be sure to record where you spend it. This will help you discover how and where you are currently spending your money. You'll be able to recognize the excess right away and see where your problem areas are.

3. **Calculate your 10/10/80 budget.** Now that you've seen where all the money is going, it's time to redirect that money into some giving, saving, and spending that will help your family rather than hurt them financially.

4. **Don't forget about the hidden bills.** These are expenses that should be figured into the monthly budget in order to give an accurate assessment of where you are in annual expenses. These include bills that may not come due on a monthly basis. Nevertheless, your budget should provide for you to have money to pay on those items when they come due. These debts also include insurance premiums, property and other taxes, retail credit, money owed to family and friends, doctor and dentist bills, vet bills, magazine subscriptions, etc. There are blank spaces on the budget work sheet to fill in these expenses.

5. **Measure your progress regularly.** Continue to keep records, and once a quarter, assess your progress toward your financial goals. Are you paying down debt? Are you giving to your community? Are you building your savings accounts?

During these evaluation sessions, you may need to reassess either your goals or your plan. And it doesn't have to be a drag! Make it a fun time—go to a local coffee shop, chow down on a baguette, sip a latte, and talk dough.

6. **No worries, mon!** When I went to Jamaica on a writer's cruise, I chose the shore excursion called zip-lining. We strapped on a harness, attached a metal loop to our belts, and rode lines attached to hundred-foot tree canopies in the jungle. The Jamaican guides would smile reassuringly and say, "No worries, mon! It will be all right!" Having a confident, relaxed view of your plan will help you to achieve your goals.

Isn't it the best feeling to know that you have the power over your money?

FINAL PROFUNDITIES

Before you purchase anything, do your homework. Research and find out what would be a good value for that particular item. Decide *ahead of time* what you will pay and stick to that amount! Don't be afraid to walk out and think about it for a week. More often than not, that outfit will still be in the store, that car will still be on the lot, and that house will still be for sale in a week's time, and you'll have the satisfaction of knowing that you didn't give in to impulse buying.

When we learn to be content with simple things, we are less likely to buy more stuff and spend beyond our means. If we simplify, we can live beneath our means, thereby having extra to save and invest. None of this will happen if we cannot catch the vision of how gratifying it can be to adopt a "less is more" view of life. The added benefit of simplifying is that we will de-stress our lives in the process.

You have to remind yourself why you're saving. Is it for personal financial freedom? To get out of debt? To save for a house? To put your kids through college? To retire early? To go on a special vacation? Write down the "whys" of your new and improved living plan and post it where you can review it regularly. Better yet, get a tangible reminder of your goal—something that will make you feel good about being diligent financially. Here are some ideas:

- **Chart.** One woman plotted her debts on a chart so she could measure how quickly she was paying off her credit card debt. Her spirit soared as she watched her balance go down.
- **Cards.** Another woman printed a card to carry in her wallet that read, "Debt Free, That's for Me!" Every time she took out her money, she saw her card and was reminded of her goals.
- **Trips.** If you want to own a dream home one day, take a free drive to some of the houses in the country or in that neighborhood where you'd like to live. What a great reminder of where you would like to be one day.

Finally—and this is the really fun part, no lie—create for yourself (and your family if you have one) a built-in, no-kidding, honest-to-goodness *splurge*. Every budget, even the tightest, needs a little wiggle room to enjoy "fun money." Devise a specific way to wisely spend this, rather than wasting it on a series of little things. You can make spending this money mandatory, if you'd like.

Use some of the tips I listed in chapter 6 on recreation and entertainment and plan that night out for dinner, a trip to the zoo, a movie night, or a visit to the amusement park. Save for a special, fabulous, yet affordable vacation that your family will remember forever. Put it on your calendar, calculate how much you need to save each week, and look forward to both long-term and short-term splurges.

Another idea is to commit smaller amounts of "found" money, such as rebates to pay for movie and dinner dates. Sure the larger windfall checks should go to reducing consumer debt, but it's perfectly all right to splurge with these special treats. A night out can help in many ways by allowing you to connect with family members, by helping you to unwind, and by reinforcing the fact that you can stay on a budget and still have a blast.

And that's it! Thanks for picking up this book. I hope you'll get the full picture of how much you can really save by picking up a copy of my companion book *Living Rich for Less* and checking out my Web site and blog at www .elliekay.com. Along with great money-saving tips, my Web site also has hundreds of calculators and tools to help with financial insight and decisions. Click on the Tool Center and check them out! Then drop me a note to tell me your story of big savings. I can't wait to hear from you!

Notes

Chapter 2: Save Big on Housing and Utilities

1. "Survey Finds Monthly Costs Outweigh Purchase Price of Home Ownership," *Mortgage News Daily,* July 7, 2006, www.mortgagenewsdaily.com/772006_Home _Ownership.asp.

2. "Rental Demand Pushes Rates Up," *Realtor Magazine,* April 22, 2008, www.realtor.org/rmodaily.nsf/f3c66d0 c6457c1e1862570af000cb13b/4aba4938c027258f862 5743300508540?OpenDocument.

3. "Is mortgage crisis causing divorces?" *MSN Money,* April 16, 2008, http://articles.moneycentral.msn.com /Banking/HomeFinancing/IsMortgageCrisisCausing Divorces.aspx

Chapter 3: Save Big on Transportation

1. "Poll: Traffic in the United States," *ABC News,* May 7, 2009, http://abcnews.go.com/Technology/Traffic /Story?id=485098&page=1.

2. "Poll: Traffic in the United States," *ABC News,* May 7, 2009, http://abcnews.go.com/Technology/Traffic /Story?id=485098&page=1.

Chapter 6: Save Big on Recreation and Entertainment

1. See Alec Gallup et al., *The Gallup Poll: Public Opinion 2005* (Lanham, MD: Rowman & Littlefield, 2007), 86,

available online at http://books.google.com/books
?id=WOug0pzW6_IC&pg=PA86&lpg=PA86&dq=
average+Americans+spend+on+recreation+entertain
ment&source=bl&ots=b2-fF3jf6K&sig=hAY8oY3
w-TTVyNU8Q1_aW6arovs&hl=en&ei=ohv1SYaoB5
CmM6zr7MsP&sa=X&oi=book_result&ct=result&res
num=2#PPA86,M1.

2. Gallup et al., *The Gallup Poll,* 86, available online at
http://books.google.com/books?id=WOug0pzW6_IC&
pg=PA86&lpg=PA86&dq=average+Americans+spend+
on+recreation+entertainment&source=bl&ots=b2-fF
3jf6K&sig=hAY8oY3w-TTVyNU8Q1_aW6arovs
&hl=en&ei=ohv1SYaoB5CmM6zr7MsP&sa=X&oi=
book_result&ct=result&resnum=2#PPA86,M1.

3. Ann Mason, "Dog Walkers: Volunteer to Walk Dogs at
Animal Shelters," *Charity Guide,* www.charityguide
.org/volunteer/fewhours/dog-walkers.htm.

4. D'Vera Cohn, "Do Parents Spend Enough Time with
Their Children?" *Population Reference Bureau,* January
2007, www.ask.com/bar?q=how+much+time+
do+parents+spend+with+their+children&page=1&qsrc
=0&ab=1&u=http%3A%2F%2Fwww.prb.org%2
FArticles%2F2007%2FDoParentsSpendEnough
TimeWithTheirChildren.aspx; Becky Barrow, "19
Minutes—How Long Working Parents Give Their
Children," *London Mail Online*, May 17, 2009,
www.ask.com/bar?q=how+much+time+do+parents+
spend+with+their+children&page=1&qsrc=0&ab=
0&u=http%3A%2F%2Fwww.dailymail.co.uk%
2Fnews%2Farticle-396609%2F19-minutes—long-
working-parents-children.html.

Chapter 8: Save Big on Gifts

1. Jennifer Waters, "Look, Ma, No Money: Times Are So Tough Even Mothers Will Get Stiffed on Their Day," *MarketWatch,* April 16, 2009, online at www.market-watch.com/story/times-so-tough-even-mom.

Chapter 9: Save Big on Medical, Dental, and Insurance

1. "Scam Alerts: Discount Medical Cards," *Coalition Against Insurance Fraud,* www.insurancefraud.org /discount_health_plans.htm.

Chapter 11: Save Big on Education

1. Regular Military Compensation Calculator, Office of the Secretary of Defense, www.defenselink.mil/ militarypay/pay/calc/index.html.
2. National Compensation Survey, March 2008. Figure represents companies employing 100 workers or more. www.bls.gov/ncs/ebs/benefits/2008/ownership/private/ table26a.pdf.
3. Neil Parmar, "Slideshow: Colleges That Pay Off," *SmartMoney,* December 16, 2008, www.smartmoney .com/Personal-Finance/College-Planning/colleges-that-pay-off.

Chapter 12: Save Big on Everything Else!

1. www.debt-elimination-guide.net/debt-to-income-ratio .html.

The 10/10/80 Budget

Account Name	Current Budget	Difference Between Current and New	New 10/10/80 Budget
Giving/Tithes/ Contributions 10 percent			
Savings 10 percent			
Spending Totals 80 percent			
Food 10 percent			
Clothing/ Dry Cleaning 5 percent			
Education/ Miscellaneous 5 percent			
Housing/Utilities/ Taxes 30 percent			
Insurance 5 percent			
Medical/Dental 4 percent			
Recreation/ Vacation/Gifts 6 percent			
Transportation 15 percent			
Net Income			

Acknowledgments

I want to thank the people who made this little book happen in a big way. First, I want to thank Ginger Kolbaba for her editorial help in completing this project in such a short time. Your professionalism, perfect sense of humor, and productivity amaze me. Suffice to say, this book would not have been written without you. To Ken Petersen and Steve Cobb at WaterBrook Press, I thank you for believing in me for the long haul, and I pray your faith in this work is rewarded. I also hope that you continue to be encouraged as you change the world in a positive way one book at a time. To Carie Freimuth, I thank you for your favor in marketing. I don't take that for granted. A hearty thanks also goes to Alice Crider for her quick edit on this project. For the team of Tiffany Lauer, Lori Addicott, and Steve Reed, I am also most grateful. I very much appreciate my publicity team of Jane Rohman and John Bianco. You're the best and have taken me to new worlds through mentoring and media! A final professional thanks goes to Steve Laube, my agent, whom I've known from the beginning. Your expanding expertise in so many different aspects of my career has been priceless. I don't think you've ever met a contract you couldn't negotiate!

To my family who puts up with short-notice deadlines, I thank you for your support. My husband, Bob, is *the* reason I am so productive (in more ways than one!). I thank you for being there to help with all the many things that you do for the kids and me. To our kiddos Daniel and Jenn, Philip, Bethany, Jonathan, Joshua, Missy, and Moran (Oriah and Eden). Your father and I reflect regularly on how incredible it is that so many above average offspring came from such incredibly average parents. We are proud of each of you. I have no greater joy than to hear that my children walk in truth.

To my friends who are there when I call, e-mail, or text. You know who you are, and I count myself rich for having you in my life. Thank you for being mighty men and women in your support of my family and work.

To the One who would rather die than live without me, the work is always for You.